Bremner!

Bremner!

The Legend of Billy Bremner

Bernard Bale

ANDRÉ DEUTSCH

First published in 1998 by
André Deutsch Limited
76 Dean Street
London WIV 5HA
www.vci.co.uk

André Deutsch is a VCI plc company

A catalogue record for this book is available from the British Library

ISBN 0 233 99446 7

Typeset by Derek Doyle & Associates
Mold, Flintshire
Printed and bound by
Werner Söderström
Osakeyhtiö in Finland

ACKNOWLEDGEMENTS

To Vicky Bremner and her family and to Issy McDonald, Alex Smith, Allan Clarke and Billy's many other friends and contemporaries for their approval and great assistance. And also to the man himself, Billy Bremner, for the inspiration he gave – even in his absence.

FOREWORD

by Alex Smith

Billy Bremner. What more can you say? When I first met him he was a wee lad pleading to be allowed to play football with us bigger and slightly older lads. He was turned down several times, but I spoke up for him and thus began a friendship that lasted to his sad passing away. That was one of Billy's many outstanding features, his undoubted loyalty. If you ever once did something for him, he never forgot it. You had a loyal friend for life.

That loyalty manifested itself in his playing career. He was fiercely loyal to both Leeds United and to Scotland. He always gave every game everything he had to offer. I knew when I first met Billy that I had met someone special. He had fantastic football ability and tremendous endurance. When he asked to play with our junior team he watched for six games before he was finally included in a match. He knew what he wanted and he was determined to achieve it.

I remember what a thrill it was for him when he played at Wembley for Scotland Schoolboys against England Schoolboys. He was tremendously proud of that, as were his family and friends. Much of his career is owed to his parents, who did their best to support him although it was not easy for them. Along with John Wynn and Dave Buchanan, they would organize Raploch street teams, so that he could play and learn from match experience. Billy never forgot that.

He was always willing to learn and to improve his game. He had played as a winger, or inside-forward, before Don Revie pulled him back to right-half. He never questioned the move, he just went along with it and gave it his best effort. That was another demonstration of his loyalty.

Part of the reason that he was homesick in his early days at Leeds was because of his feelings for his friends and family. In a sense he felt that he had deserted them and he wanted to be back with them. But they did not feel deserted and were always encouraging to him. A key time in his life was when he met Vicky who later became his wife. She was tremendous for him and together with their children, Billy, Donna and Amanda, they carved a wonderful life.

People often thought of Billy Bremner as being a little guy. He wasn't! He might have only been 5ft 6ins in height, but he was a very big guy. If Billy was in the room it did not matter how crowded it was, you could never miss him. He always had such tremendous character and presence that his personality towered above everyone else.

One of the things that always amazed me was his incredible leadership quality. With Leeds United he was among players like Johnny Giles, Jack Charlton, Norman Hunter and others, all great players who were leaders themselves. It was the same in the Scotland camp with Billy McNeill, Dave Mackay, John Greig – with whom Billy often roomed – and the rest. Yet they were all prepared to follow this magnetic man from Stirling wherever he chose to take them.

Billy oozed confidence. He always said that he never took the field feeling inferior to anyone else on the pitch. His positive play and leadership qualities demonstrated that.

I had the great privilege of playing alongside him, but I had the even greater privilege of knowing him and being counted among his close friends. I was there when he began, I was there when he had his proudest football moments, I was best man when he was married, and I was there when we all said farewell to him.

What a career he had. What a life he had. Billy Bremner . . . what a man he was!

INTRODUCTION

I cannot recall exactly when I first met Billy Bremner. It was sometime before the famous FA Cup Final of 1965. We met occasionally during the years that followed, but it was during the time of his so-called retirement that we most often chatted. Billy liked to reminisce, but he also liked to discuss the game of football both of yesterday and today – with not just a little attention paid to the game of tomorrow. He was vibrant company and always had plenty to say. He was not one of those former players who thought that today's game was hopeless. He gave credit where it was due and handed out the brickbats where he felt they were deserved.

In this book the reader will find many quotes collected from our various conversations, misspent afternoons in Billy's garden where the coffee and football talk flowed as freely as the waterfall into his ornamental fish-pond.

Billy Bremner talked as he played football, always with his heart and soul. Whenever he had something to say you knew that you were listening to much more than idle opinion. Here was a man who had been there and done it – and done it spectacularly well. He was always prepared to listen, though, probably a hangover from his days as a young man when he knew that it paid to listen to the words of his mentor, Don Revie.

Physically, Billy Bremner is no longer with us, for now at least. But while he may be suspended for a while you just know that he will be back in explosive action, an even better player than before.

1

BROCK IN RAPLOCH

We sat in the lounge with tea, biscuits and some slices of cake
that his wife, Vicky, had provided. We talked about football, of
course, although there was an interruption when a neighbour's
security alarm suddenly leaped into action, triggered by the
invasion of small flies that had descended upon the village as
if determined to make the oppressive heat even more unbear-
able. Billy was up and out of the door in a flash – he knew that
his neighbours were away and that there was no one at home
at the time. It was a telling moment.

Billy had been sitting in front of a glass cabinet filled to
capacity with just some of the many trophies and honours
handed out to him during his career as a professional footballer. He was relaxed – possibly a bit overweight and
definitely a little over-indulgent with the cigarettes. He looked
happy and he smiled a lot. He occasionally allowed a hand to
brush his silver hair as he reflected on something that rankled
a little from a game long gone. His eyes gleamed and his body
twitched with pent-up excitement as he became animated over
some point or other.

Now and then he would allow the conversation to stray to
his Jaguar car, the family pony, the best way to travel to
Swansea, his grandson or even religion. Perhaps this was not
the Billy Bremner, the passionate Scotsman who could lead
men across the Sahara, up Everest, and through the frozen
wastes of the bottom division. Perhaps this man was his uncle,

a relaxed elder statesman who preferred carpet slippers and a night in by the fire.

Yet in a moment he would be off and running again, back on the football track. Once again his eye would gleam and his body would twitch with the excitement of games remembered and points scored. Yes, this was the same Billy Bremner who had been the heart and soul of Leeds United during their finest hours. The same Billy Bremner who would run and run and run for ninety hours, let alone ninety minutes, for the sheer delight of playing football. I was in the presence of one of the greatest footballers who ever lived, a smoking volcano of passion and energy, proud of his profession and proud of his roots. He loved his Scottish heritage.

'It really annoys me when they call me an Anglo-Scot,' he told me. 'I've as much Scottish blood pumping through my veins as anyone still living in Scotland. I have shed blood, sweat and tears for my country and I am proud to have done so. And I'll tell you this too – I would do it all over again, anytime, anywhere! Anglo-Scot indeed. I'm a Scotsman and don't anyone dare forget it.'

On 9 December 1942 the Bremner household was blessed with the arrival of a son named William John. Football was a major preoccupation in the Raploch district of Stirling. Everyone was well aware that there was a war on, of course, but in a tough area like Raploch, there had always been a war on.

Billy's father, James, was a man of enterprise. He was a coal-man most of the time but he also sold newspapers on street corners and ran one of the local junior football teams. Billy's mother, Bridget, better known as Bess, was a typical Scottish mother hen, a warm provider for her family and anyone else's who might be in need. She was gentle but in just an instant her eyes would flash, and woe betide anyone taking liberties with her or her family.

To the locals of Raploch, James Bremner was always known affectionately as 'Pop', and that affection was deeply sincere.

He rarely had anything but a kind word for anyone. He loved football and knew the game well. At the drop of a hat he would demonstrate some move or other to the kids in the street and they would eagerly listen to what he said, and they certainly learned.

Among those kids, of course, was his own son Billy. Naturally, he was the primary subject of his father's coaching skills. Billy never missed an opportunity to place the majority of his success at his father's feet. Not only did he encourage Billy and teach him all the basic skills, but he set him on the road to stardom with sound advice.

Young Billy lived in a three-room council house at 35A Weir Street. Being a little chap, Billy knew what it was like to be the victim of attempted bullying. I say 'attempted' because nobody ever really got the better of him. He was a thinking lad who liked people and hated to see anyone taken for granted. His friends included Tony Lafferty, Alex Smith, John Hogg, Ian 'Carrots' Pow and Benny McGuire; Issy Lafferty was his best pal. Now Issy McDonald, she was a close friend of Billy, and later his family, throughout his life. She was also a tremendous footballer and explained how Billy Bremner became known as 'Brock'.

'I was a left winger and, though I say it myself, I had a better left foot than Gray or Lorimer. I would have loved to play for the school alongside Billy, but since I was a girl that was never possible. However, we had our own team and Billy and I were team-mates. I was nicknamed "Stella", and Billy became "Brock" when we played at the local swing park on Sundays. We used to meet up with other youngsters and split into teams. Each team put a shilling in the hat and whoever won the most games used to take all the cash – the money came from returned pop bottles and odd jobs. Billy's favourite expression was, "Are we going for broke?" With his accent it sounded like Brock and that's how he got his nickname. I don't ever remember us losing a game so we did all right out of it.'

Issy also had a good playing career as she was in great

demand to play for various ladies' teams and was even capped by Scotland. She then went on to manage the very successful and well-known Raploch Boys' Club side. Her daughter, Wendy, is a goalkeeper with Stirling Albion Ladies, who have moved from the Fourth Division into the Premier Division in just four seasons. She has also become a member of the Scotland Ladies' squad. Issy and Billy were connected by family in that Billy's grandmother was Issy's aunt – but the football influence stems from their close friendship.

As well as football, Billy also enjoyed swimming in the local river, cycling and walking. He and his pals were as near as you could ever get to Enid Blyton's Famous Five. Billy Bremner also had a sweet tooth. He liked Mars bars and rhubarb rock, and something else which almost landed him in trouble several times. Here, for the first time, I can reveal that Billy's love of toffee apples nearly lured him into a life of crime.

'We all liked toffee apples, but Billy really loved them,' Issy McDonald recalled. 'There was a neighbour of Billy's, Mr Wheater, who used to make them and sell them around the streets in a barrow. He used to put them on his window sill to set. Billy, my brother Tony and I used to take it in turns to climb up the drainpipe after we had seen him go out, and help ourselves. To this day that man never knew who was the mystery toffee-apple burglar!'

Billy was also partial to Duncan's Limeade Juice, so we can see where all those football winnings were spent.

I'd like a fiver for every time that I have heard some famous football icon say that they started kicking a ball as soon as they could walk. But however often you hear it, it is probably true and, in the case of Billy Bremner, it definitely was. He didn't just learn to kick the ball. He had learned very early on that no one gives you the ball gift-wrapped – you have to take it your-self. Family kickabouts quickly became competitive and, by the time that Billy began to play in organized school games, he was already well versed in tackling, passing and possession. He also knew about shooting and heading. Billy Bremner's pre-school education was all about football. Before he had even heard of the 'three Rs' he was learning football's 'three Cs' – control, confidence and competitiveness.

If there was ever any doubt about Billy's prospects in the game it was because of his size – or lack of it. He was a little lad in both height and width. Yet he was never still as he energized even the St Mary's Primary School team, for whom he first kicked a ball in anger. However, onlookers, mesmerized by the skill of a boy far advanced in the finer arts of football, would often shake their heads and say, 'What a pity he's not a wee bit bigger.' They had forgotten, of course, that there is a difference between size and stature.

At St Modan's Secondary School, Billy proved to be an excellent pupil. Occasionally a classroom fidget, he nevertheless committed himself to the job in hand and was a willing student. He enjoyed his lessons, although he was sometimes reprimanded for gazing a little imprudently out of the window – perhaps daydreaming of playing football for Scotland. From an early age Billy dreamed of football, both day and night. His heroes wore the dark blue shirts of his country. It mattered little to him what their domestic colours might be.

He was taken to see football matches in both the local park and at the two major local grounds – Firs Park and Annfield Park, where East Stirling and Stirling Albion plied their part-time trades. There were also those special excursions to Glasgow – trips which Billy was soon making on his own, as he recalled.

'I loved going to both Ibrox and Parkhead. I favoured Celtic, but it didn't really matter that much to me. I just loved being among the vast crowds watching the very cream of Scottish football,' said Billy. 'Celtic and Rangers were at home on alternate Saturdays, so I could go every week and watch some of my heroes. I cheered them all on and enjoyed every minute from the moment I left home to the time when I fell asleep in my bed later that night. Those were marvellous days.'

Although he was a Catholic and mostly followed Celtic, Billy never subscribed to the religious divide that has caused so much heartache through the centuries. He remained a

Catholic all his life despite the occasional doubt. Sometimes, while away on international duty, he would have a wander around a Catholic church or cathedral.

'I was always left with more questions than answers,' he told me. 'It always seemed to me that the Catholic buildings were at their most ornate in countries which could least afford them.'

Billy's heroes during those early years of his football education were drawn from both sides of that religious divide, but they were often united in the dark blue shirt of Scotland, a shirt which Billy himself dreamed of wearing one day.

'I used to think about football all the time, and I used to daydream about playing for Scotland. When we played in the street or in the playground I always imagined that I was in a Scotland shirt, and that it was a do-or-die situation. I could hear the crowd urging us on. If I was just daydreaming as I walked along the road, or before I fell asleep at night, or even in the classroom, I used to see myself scoring a winning goal – sometimes a long shot which sent the ball thundering into the net, sometimes a run through a crowd of defenders, and sometimes a great header. The more I daydreamed the more I tried to make it happen.

'My father used to remind me very often that things did not just happen, you had to work hard to make them happen. He was a great help to me, I could not have wished for greater support from my parents. They were always encouraging and never minded that I was completely mad about football. I think they were just as mad about it themselves really!'

Bremner's soccer knowledge went further than Celtic, Rangers, or his two local Stirling clubs, however.

'There was another team in my life and I followed them avidly. I was always fascinated by their name even though I had no idea where they played. All I knew was that they had a great name and, because of that, they must be a great team to play for. That team was Exeter City and I found them in the football results when I was still a wee boy. I took interest in them from that moment on. Years later I went to their ground and I felt like a pilgrim must have felt when he finally arrived at the place he had been seeking.'

Among Bremner's heroes was George Young – 'Corky' as he became known after he kept the cork from a champagne bottle as a souvenir of his part in the Rangers' Scottish Cup triumph of 1948. Bremner admired Young for his uncompromising style.

'On the pitch he looked massive. It was not just that he was a big guy physically, he was also so very imposing. To me he was one of the greatest defenders that Scotland had ever produced. Even though I was really a Celtic fan, I could not help but admire this great Rangers defender. He was a giant of a man in every sense of the word and I found him to be very inspiring. I knew I could never be like him in size – but I could do my very best to play like him.'

Eric Caldow was another of Billy's heroes. Like George Young he played for both Rangers and Scotland and captained both. What was so special about him?

'He was such a great captain. He was the sort of player who inspired those around him. He was strong in the tackle but he was also as quick as a winger in launching a counter-attack. He had a quick brain and great vision. He was simply a brilliant player who never gave up and kept his team-mates going for the full ninety minutes.'

Billy Bremner's most inspirational hero was Bobby Collins, who played for Celtic in the early 1950s and was another Scottish international.

'What a player Bobby was. I used to love to go and watch him. I suppose I could relate closely to him because he was a little guy like me. When I used to see him when I was a lad, he was doing all that I had dreamed of. He was wearing the Celtic shirt and he was capped by Scotland from 1951 onwards. He controlled the game from midfield. I thought he was fantastic and if I ever wanted to be someone else it would have been Bobby Collins. It was a great honour for me when I later played alongside him.'

As Bremner related his memories of his football heroes, he

was still, in a sense, in awe of them. He was still a fan – a fan who did not seem to realize that he had not only emulated their skills and achievements but had, in many ways, over-hauled and surpassed their feats.

With heroes like George Young, Eric Caldow and Bobby Collins, it is not difficult to see how Billy Bremner's play was styled in so many ways in those tender years when he was a regular visitor to Celtic Park, Ibrox and Hampden. Yet he was always his own man and never once tried to be a clone of those whom he admired so much.

'I never tried to be the same as any of those great players. I did learn from watching them and I would try to copy some of the things they did, but I never imagined myself to be one of them. I think that can inhibit your own natural style of play. Watching kids over the last decade, I have grown increasingly worried that youngsters spend far too much time trying to pose and look the same as their heroes and not enough time in actually learning to play the game their own way. Watching some lads in the park I noticed that they went through the motions of well-rehearsed goal celebrations when one of them scored in a casual kickabout. Yet not one of them could kick the ball properly.'

In his earliest school games Bremner quietly gained a repu-tation as a livewire with all the energy and zest of a young colt let loose into a field after days cooped up in a stable. While all the other kids were still sorting out which was their right leg and which was their left, young Billy was already capably passing from one to the other.

His ball control was a direct product of his father's tuition and his own constant practice. There are only a very few play-ers who can truly live up to the term 'a natural', but Billy was one of them. Make no mistake, he worked very hard to get the best from his talent, but he had the necessary confidence from a very early age.

At school he was playing alongside boys who were both older and bigger than he was, but he was never concerned or fazed by his opposition. In those early days his whole outlook was being moulded at the same time as his very definite abilities. By the time he was in his early teens he was already playing for Gowanhill, a Scottish junior side, in which all his team-mates were twice his size and at least seven years older.

'I soon discovered one thing about playing against lads who were twice as big as me,' said Billy. 'I had to make up for my lack of height and weight by getting stuck in just that little bit harder. And it's a funny thing, you know, when you come up against a big fellow and he doesn't realize that you have this streak of steel inside of you, he's a bit apt to think that you're going to be a pushover. That is, until that first real tackle – then he suddenly starts to realize that, even if you haven't got the brawn, you do possess quite a bite!

'Anyway, if I did form any bad habits around that time – and there are a lot of people around who have assured me that I did – there was one thing which became the most important that I have ever learned. Never give anything less than 100 per cent – in everything that you decide to do. If you want to come out on top of the heap you have to try that little bit harder than the next fellow or you will never make it.'

Alex Smith, who went on to become one of Scotland's most famous names as both a player and a manager, recalled young Billy's tenacity against the bigger lads.

'We were training in the park when Billy turned up on a bike. It was an old grey bike, a girl's bike. He asked if he could play but he was turned down because of his size. He just kept on coming to watch and asking if he could play. There was an old man, Willie Gordon, who ran the team at that time, and once he had seen Billy play he signed him right away, but it took some convincing for Billy to get a game. In the end I asked if maybe we could let him play on the wing and then he would stay out of trouble. I was Billy's pal for life after that. When he got hold of the ball, the rest of us might just as well have gone home. We couldn't get near him. That was it – he was never refused again.'

Issy McDonald remembers that old grey bike well.

'It was a girl's bike. Billy borrowed it. I think he meant to ask her but he forgot – he was in such a hurry to get to the football.'

That sounds just like Billy Bremner. Football always came first!

2

OFF TO SEE THE WORLD

St Modan's fame for football reached way beyond the area of Stirling and, by the time Billy got into his final year of schooling, he had succeeded in getting into the Scotland boys' team. In that particular season he played in four international games. He was in that team with many team-mates who have since achieved recognition and fame, and many of those whom he played against became equally famous.

Terry Venables, Phil Chisnall, Ronnie Boyce, Bert Murray and Jantzen Derrick of England played, as did Jimmy Nicholson of Northern Ireland and Barry Hole of Wales. The Scottish team had an impressive forward line that season consisting of Andy Penman, Tommy Henderson, Ian Gibson, Billy himself, and Bobby Hope. There is no doubt that, at today's astronomical transfer fees, that particular line-up would be well out of range of any club's finances.

No one in that Scottish forward line stood much above five feet in their football boots and, when the team lined up against England at Wembley, Billy's own words were, 'They're a lot of bloody giants!'

In that game against England, Tommy Henderson did the almost unpardonable by missing a penalty. However, it was just one of those things and it made no difference at all to the friendship that existed between him and Billy Bremner. Football-daft, they were the best of pals in the Scotland boys' team and, just before leaving school, they made a pact to stick with each other whatever might happen in the future.

11

Accordingly, when they set out on their search for football fame and fortune, it was together.

'Tommy and I had become inseparable. We were like two peas in a pod and could not have been closer if we had been brothers. We used to spend all our spare time kicking a ball about and, to us, it would be quite a natural development to join the same football club, if such a thing should happen at all.'

Following their appearances with the Scotland boys' team they were both invited down to see Arsenal and Chelsea. They spent a fortnight in London, savouring the sights and sounds of the big city and enjoying the hospitality of those two famous clubs. By the end of their stay both of the clubs had offered them terms. Naturally excited by the offers, they returned back home to think things over.

News of Bremner's talent had travelled far and wide, and with good reason, as Alex Smith recalled.

'He was exceptional, and everyone who saw him play knew that they were watching a star of the future. I remember once we were going to play on a pitch covered in snow – and I mean several inches thick. Only the lines had been cleared. I said to Billy, "You're going to have trouble doing your stuff on this pitch!" It wasn't long before he had scored from thirty yards.

'He always had such a positive approach, even as a young-ster, but he never expected anything to be easy. From an early age he realized that hard work and honest effort were the keys to success. I remember just after he had signed for Leeds and I had been given a contract by Kilmarnock, we went down to Hampden to see the Real Madrid–Eintracht Frankfurt European Cup Final. We stood at the Mount Florida end, totally enthralled by the football education we were receiving. At the end of it, Billy turned to me and said, "We've got a mountain to climb." He recognized the path that lay ahead to make it to the top of football.'

There was another club interested in Billy Bremner, but they missed out for what to Billy was a very puzzling reason, as Issy McDonald revealed.

'Rangers were very interested in him. They watched him and then they talked to him and they were obviously very impressed. Then they discovered that Billy was a Catholic and they disappeared into the sunset. Billy himself never considered that religion and football had anything in common, so he didn't really understand what the problem was. He didn't let it trouble him though. He just shrugged his shoulders and got on with his life.'

However, the offers didn't end there. On the week following their return from London, Celtic came into the picture and invited Billy and Tommy down to Parkhead for a spell of training. Then, just as they had decided to accept that offer, yet another club came on the scene, Leeds United. The manager there, Bill Lambton, and the chairman, Harry Reynolds, had travelled up to Scotland to meet the two young players after seeing them on television when they had played against England.

Young Billy Bremner, who knew little of the clubs south of the border, had never even heard of Leeds as a city, let alone as a football club. He knew, of course, about the well-known clubs such as Manchester United and Tottenham Hotspur and, following his trip to London, he now knew all about Chelsea and Arsenal, but Leeds was a completely unknown quantity. Tommy Henderson, who was perhaps better acquainted with the geography of the British Isles, was able to put him straight. Billy asked him, 'Who the hell are they? Are they in the Fourth Division or something?' Tommy laughed and said: 'Dinna be stupid . . . they're in the First Division of course!'

First Division or not – what really clinched the trip down to Leeds was the fact that the lads were beginning to enjoy their trips up and down the length of Britain. The trips were all at someone else's expense and they were getting the red-carpet treatment from all those famous managers and players that they had heard about but had never expected to meet. To both Billy and Tommy, another holiday at Leeds United's expense was far preferable to remaining at home – even if staying at home would have meant a day's training with Celtic.

13

Young Billy Bremner liked the straightforward approach and down-to-earth manner of Harry Reynolds. That was probably the main reason that a deal was finally struck. Despite Leeds United not being the most fashionable of teams and certainly being an unknown quantity as far as the two lads were concerned, it wasn't too long before they were persuaded to sign for the club.

'I was quite taken with being in demand. As well as Arsenal and Chelsea, there was interest from Sheffield Wednesday and Aston Villa. It was quite flattering. The truth is that I really wanted to join Celtic and I was hoping that they would make a firm bid before any of the others did. My father had other ideas. He told me quite plainly that he was not going to have me get caught up with any religious controversy – and that automatically ruled out Celtic because of the sectarianism between them and Rangers. "You're going to England, and that's that." I could never argue with my father. I could try, but he always had the last word.'

Almost immediately the boys began to regret their hasty decision. In those days Leeds United was not the club that it is today – in fact, far from it. It wasn't long before both Tommy and Billy were really fed up. Yorkshire was a world away from the Scotland that they both knew and homesickness was beginning to aggravate their problems. They made no secret of their feelings either, which proved to be unsettling for the people around them and so, finally, they were both called into the office of the general manager, Cyril Wilkinson. He gave them a serious talking to in a vain attempt to sort out the problem.

'What Cyril Wilkinson did not know was that Tommy and I had made a pact that if we did not at least get into the reserves by the end of the season we would leave and go back to Scotland. We were two very ambitious fifteen-year-olds and, since we knew that other clubs had been interested, we thought that we could afford to have such an attitude.'

Tommy Henderson's mind was made up and he was fully determined to leave and go back to Scotland. Billy Bremner had decided to join him in a double walk-out – that is until he received some welcome news. He had been selected for the reserve team and would be playing at Preston on the following Wednesday!

That sudden promotion from apparent obscurity changed everything for Billy Bremner. Gone was the boredom and the homesickness – at least for the present. He decided to give himself a little bit longer to try to settle in at Leeds United – Tommy Henderson would have to return home alone.

'Tommy and I did not fall out over the fact that he was going and I was staying. We both understood each other well enough and we parted as good pals and kept in touch. Tommy went on to play for Celtic and for Hearts and, ironically, he was later signed for Leeds by Don Revie. We remained good friends.'

Billy committed himself to staying at Leeds for another year, but it was a year that remained unhappy and the absence of his close friend made it all the more difficult to bear. Once again, as the year came to an end, he resolved to return to Scotland.

It almost seems that someone must have been watching closely and had learned from the first occasion when Bremner was about to return home. Just when his desire to leave had reached its peak, a little piece of information was leaked. Quite out of the blue he heard that there was a chance – just a chance – that he would be selected for the first team to play against Chelsea. Whoever that psychologist on the Elland Road staff was, it is a fact that his action gave Bremner the necessary nudge which led him on to such fame and fortune with Leeds United. Pining though he was to return home, Bremner was sensible enough to realize that if opportunity was indeed knocking, he just could not afford to miss out on his chance.

To Bremner's great joy the rumour proved to be true and, just a month or so after his seventeenth birthday, he made his League debut against Chelsea at Stamford Bridge. His chance came because Chris Crowe had been injured and Billy was put in on the wing to partner Don Revie. Revie made sure that his new partner received a chance to gain some of the limelight that day and that helped the young Billy Bremner to appreciate more fully the qualities of the man who was later to become one of the world's top managers and, in particular, his boss at Elland Road.

Right from the start, Don Revie took Bremner under his wing. It was as if he realized the young player's mood of uncertainty. He arranged for them to room together in the London hotel, made sure that they were in bed early, and that they were up again at seven the next morning for a long walk before the streets became filled with car exhaust fumes. All of the time that they were together he talked about nothing but football. All of Revie's vast experience was paraded for the benefit of the young Billy Bremner.

Billy's debut was on 23 January 1960, and it was quite a match at Stamford Bridge. Leeds were enjoying a mini-revival after going through the first half of a season in which they had suffered far too many defeats for comfort.

'I don't think any player ever really forgets his debut. I wore a No. 7 shirt and before the kick-off I looked around and could see famous faces everywhere. Once the game started, though, I forgot about that, and it was not until it was all over that I once again took in the fact that I had been playing football in the First Division surrounded by internationals. We won the game 3–1, so you can imagine how I felt once it was all over. Noel Peyton scored one and John McCole hit two. McCole had only been with Leeds since the previous September and, like myself, he was a Scot. He ended up as top scorer for the season and he was another player whom I looked upon as a bit of a hero.

'I was delighted with that win at Chelsea for more than one reason. Not only was it a brilliant start to my career to be on the winning side but I had also had a reasonable game – which, I thought, might earn me at least another chance in the first team. It was also a bit of a response to Chelsea who, I had discovered, like Arsenal, had not come back for me after the trials because they had considered me to be too small to make a professional footballer. Well, I hadn't been too small that day! Many players have been written off in the past for being too small. It was a lesson I learned very early in life and later, when

I became a manager, I never ruled out a player because of his size.'

Billy Bremner remained in the first team for the following Wednesday in a friendly game against Hull City and then, on the following Saturday, came his home debut. The Elland Road match was against West Bromwich Albion and the visitors ran riot, ending Leeds' excellent run by inflicting a 4–1 defeat. Billy missed the next couple of games, which included a 5–0 defeat at Fulham, but when he came back he continued to make progress. There was a memorable game for him on 19 March when he was named in the side that entertained Manchester City.

There was another young lad in that game who had just joined City and was making his debut for them: Denis Law. It turned out to be Bremner's day as Leeds won 4–3 but, both for himself and Law, it was a match to remember since they both scored their first goals for their respective clubs.

'Denis and I grew up together in the Scotland camp although he was a little older than me. We were great team-mates but we had some real battles on the pitch when we were in opposite camps. He always remained one of my favourite players, however, no matter what shirt he was wearing.'

Denis Law remembers that game as well.

'I haven't got the best of memories but I remember that game all right. Billy was like a little demon. He was everywhere all at the same time. I was a young lad myself and he certainly impressed me. I think everyone thought that his energy came from the excitement of youth, but he always played like that until the day he retired. We thought we had done enough to win that day, but Leeds just got the edge and beat us. Billy shook hands with me afterwards and we congratulated each other on scoring. I don't know why we did that, neither of us could stand the opposition scoring. I think that was the only time it ever happened.'

Despite his debut and relative success, Billy remained unhappy at Elland Road. At the end of his debut season Leeds were relegated, but that had nothing to do with his unhappy frame of mind. Later he put it down to not really knowing his own mind, but at the time he was still pining for Scotland. The unhappiness and uncertainty continued to affect his attitude until after he had passed his twentieth birthday.

By the time that Bremner put in his first serious transfer request, Don Revie had taken over as Leeds United manager. Walter Galbraith, then manager of Hibernian, put in an offer of £25,000 for Billy and he eagerly began to look forward to a return to his homeland. Unfortunately for Billy, Leeds decided that they could not possibly part with him for anything less than £30,000. Hibernian would not come up with the extra money and the two clubs never came to terms, so Bremner was forced to remain exactly where he was. In many ways it was fortunate, in that by being forced to stay with Leeds United, Bremner was there as the tide really began to turn.

'When I asked for a transfer soon after Don Revie became manager, it was not in any way anything to do with him personally. It was just that I felt I could not wait for regular first-team football and I was also still a bit homesick. As it happened, Hibernian had put in a £25,000 bid for me. I was obviously very excited at the prospect of a return to Scottish football with such a fine club. My new boss had other ideas, though, and he shrewdly told Hibs that the price had to be £30,000. He knew that they could not possibly afford that and the whole deal fell through. I was disappointed – but not for long. Revie was a great man-manager and soon knew how to humour me – even though he must have been sick of hearing me moan. We did not fall out over it. He had to do the best for his club and I could hardly say that he ruined my career!'

With Billy's hero, Bobby Collins, signed by Leeds, and Don Revie as manager, the rest of the team had plenty of encouragement. Leeds began to soar up the table. From being down among the dead men of the Second Division the club began an inexorable climb. By the end of the season they just missed going back into the First Division – the bad start to the season proved to be just too much for them to catch up on their rivals.

The following season was a different proposition, though, as Leeds United won promotion. Success seemed to follow, with of course the odd disappointment along the way – but before that success came, there was a lot of hard work to be done in order to get Leeds United firmly established on the soccer map. Billy Bremner did not make it easy for manager Don Revie either. In fact there were times when a lesser man would have given up on him. Billy himself said that there must have been times when 'the boss' was heartily fed up with him – sick of the sight and sound of him. And Billy couldn't blame him if he was!

Don Revie had been around a bit by the time he joined Leeds United as a player; Leicester, Hull, Manchester City, Sunderland – he was used to the footballing circuit, and he had earned himself quite a reputation as a player. He had collected a 'Footballer of the Year' award, become famous as the mainspring of the 'Revie Plan' when he was with Manchester City, and finally, he had joined Leeds.

Bremner, unaware at that time that this was the man who would lead Leeds United to such great heights, was unimpressed. Although he was grateful for the tips and advice he was given, he never really imagined that it was anything more than an old hand passing on tips to a soccer-mad youngster. Then, suddenly, Revie became manager.

Almost overnight Revie had to make the transition from being one of the boys to being the boss. The way he did it is a mark of the man himself. The players, Bremner included, were already wondering if the appointment would make for better team spirit, or whether the new boss would start to wield the big stick. Don Revie, as was his nature, took everything in his stride. He called all the players together and explained the situation to them as he saw it. He was no longer one of the boys in the dressing room – his domain was the office. His position had changed and he no longer thought it advisable to be referred to as 'Don'. However, in view of the close contact everyone had enjoyed he didn't want to be called 'Mr Revie' either. In the future, he told everyone, he would prefer to be known as 'Boss'. It is the title by which almost all professional footballers refer to their manager and so that suited the Leeds players. In fact, from that day only one player made the mistake of not referring to him as he desired.

Billy Bremner recalled the incident.

'John Charles was the player who forgot. Big John, who had won star billing with Leeds, had been transferred to Italy, and was then signed by Leeds United again from Juventus. We were travelling on the team coach one day when John turned round and addressed a question to "the Boss". Probably without thinking, John said, "What about this, Don?"

'You could have heard a pin drop – the rest of us were amazed. We waited, but the manager didn't rush in either to remind John of his title or to answer the question. "The Boss" remained silent. No one ever called him "Don" again!'

Billy was at his most unsettled at the time Don Revie became manager of Leeds United. Nearly every day he would approach Revie, pleading with him, demanding, trying to convince him that it would be much better for him and the club if he could go back to Scotland. Bremner never let a chance go by without coming up with some excuse for Revie to let him go. It got so bad that desperate measures were needed.

Don Revie must have pondered deeply on the question and finally, unknown to Billy Bremner, he took the bull by the horns and set out to solve the problem once and for all.

Billy had a girlfriend, Vicky, who worked in a factory in Stirling in Scotland. Without Billy knowing anything about it, Don Revie took it upon himself to get in his car and drive up to Scotland to see Vicky and talk about some of the problems that her suitor was posing at Leeds. Such a dramatic step on the part of Don Revie illustrates how highly he valued Billy Bremner's contribution.

Revie reached Vicky and outlined the situation to her. He explained all his plans for Leeds United, including the part that he expected Billy to play in the development of those plans. Even then, when Leeds United were still in the soccer doldrums, he was able to look ahead with vision to the day when the club would be a real power in the land.

Revie was always a good talker and he was soon able to convince Vicky that Billy would be doing himself a real disservice if he did have his way and left Leeds United. His eloquence enlisted her aid and she began to use her powers of persuasion on Billy to think about settling down in Yorkshire, and about giving the team a real try. Between them they accomplished the job so well that Billy began to think that he must be the only one marching out of step. Gradually the lectures from manager and girlfriend began to work. Bremner started to concentrate more and more on becoming a top-class footballer, and less and less on returning to Scotland. The day finally came when he and Vicky got married and set up their home together in Leeds. The happiness they shared together proved beyond a doubt that Don Revie had been right to stick his neck out and make that journey up to Scotland.

Of course, Billy Bremner wasn't the only one with whom Don Revie had problems and whom he had to handle with care in those early days. Jack Charlton wasn't exactly a 'yes man' either. Like Bremner, Jack also spent a great deal of time trying to get away from Elland Road. He made himself quite a bit of a nuisance in the process too, just like Bremner. In fact, Big Jack has since described himself as 'a one-man awkward squad'.

When Don Revie was still a player he had turned on Jack and told him quite bluntly: 'If I were a manager, I wouldn't have you in my team!' Another time, when he was manager of Leeds United, Revie told him: 'You would be playing for England at centre-half, if only you had the sense to do yourself and your club justice!'

There was a time when Charlton was ready to feud and fight with almost anyone who crossed his path – and Jack Charlton is a big man. Then, finally, Charlton, like Billy Bremner, began to feel that perhaps after all there was a future for Leeds United and the players there. Charlton had been at odds with club, manager, coaching and training staff. He had been on the verge of moving until a transfer deal had finally failed to materialize. He stayed with Leeds and became the number-one choice at

21

centre-half for his club and for his country. That World Cup winner's medal he collected will always serve as a reminder to him that Don Revie hadn't been far from the truth on the day that he had told him: 'You would be playing for England, if only ...'

The examples of Jack Charlton and Billy Bremner go to show just how difficult the job of a manager is. The problems Revie had in his early days in the job show what a difficult path he had to tread. It also shows just how much a player owes to a manager who both cares and understands what makes his players tick. Billy Bremner was one player who never forgot what he owed to Don Revie, always realizing that he would probably never have achieved such fame and fortune had it not been for the patience and dedication of that one man.

3

EARLY DAYS AT ELLAND ROAD

The real turning point for Leeds United and Billy Bremner came in the 1963/64 season. Encouraged by having finished fifth in the Second Division at the end of the previous campaign, Leeds were full of confidence when they began their promotion drive. Billy was as enthusiastic as ever and had already become a favourite with the supporters. They were not the only admiring spectators either. Scouts from several other clubs had been to see this flame-haired revelation, but Don Revie refused even to consider a bid. He was putting a team together to beat these so-called bigger clubs at their own game and he was not about to allow a major piece of his collection to go to the opposition.

The signing of Bobby Collins in March 1962 had been a masterstroke. His presence had made an immediate impact on the side. He even scored on his debut and, in the remaining eleven games of the season, Leeds had suffered only one defeat. The following season he was instrumental in turning Leeds from a team struggling in the Second Division to a side on the hunt for promotion. He cemented the team, as Billy Bremner recalled.

'Bobby was a £25,000 signing from Everton. It was a good deal for them because I don't think they lost a penny on the deal – and for us it was a brilliant signing because we knew what a difference it would make to the squad. For me in partic-ular it was a fantastic signing. I had long been a big fan of

Bobby Collins and to have him actually playing at Leeds was a tremendous boost for me.

'I was doing all right with my football, and I had a great relationship with the other players – even though they did call me "Chalky" because of the contrast between my red hair and my white complexion. However, I did have a discipline problem. I was always losing my temper and having a go at people and I was always getting into trouble for arguing with referees. I was often told about it by various people and I was getting my share of fines and suspensions – but I just couldn't help it.

'Bobby Collins was the best professional I have ever known. He was thirty-one when he joined us and everyone else was writing him off, but he stayed for several years and he played at the top of his game throughout. Even when he was seriously injured he came bouncing back to lead us to new heights. All the young players who were around at the time owed Bobby Collins a big debt for his generalship, his advice and his example.

'Whenever he was in the side I felt confident that he would bully, coax, cajole, cool us down whenever we were in danger of losing our heads, encourage and praise us whenever we did anything good, and generally look after us like a father. In the heat of the game he would sense when we were beginning to need a bit of breathing space and he would go into the fight for possession of the ball, plonk a pass upfield for Albert Johanneson to chase, while we at the back breathed a little less hard and pulled ourselves together.

'When Bobby went out to play, nothing could put him off his game. He left all his cares behind him in the dressing room and, for the next ninety minutes, only one thing mattered – that everyone should be pulling his guts out for the whole of the game in a tremendous team effort. Typical of the man was the time we were staying in a Harrogate hotel just before a game with Burnley and a plate-glass door was accidentally broken. Bobby's arm was badly gashed and a lesser man would have pulled out of the game. Bobby not only played but he scored two goals too as we won 5–1. We were battling for promotion at the time and he was determined not to miss the game. I will always remember that when we clamoured round him to congratulate him on his first goal, he kept yelling, "Mind my arm! Mind my arm!"

'I learned many great lessons from Bobby Collins, not the least being able to take the knocks as well as hand them out, and always play the game as a man. They say that one man does not make a team – but Bobby Collins came nearer to doing it than anyone else that I have ever seen on a football field.'

The presence of Bobby Collins on the pitch and in training was just the inspiration needed, but there was another man to whom Billy Bremner always paid tribute: Johnny Giles. It was another of those surprise signings when Giles was transferred from Manchester United to Second Division Leeds United for £33,000 in August 1963, and he and Bremner went on to form one of the greatest midfield partnerships ever to run onto a football pitch. Bremner became a Johnny Giles fan instantly.

'We clicked almost immediately. Somehow we knew instantly what the other would do and we were able to work together without even talking about it. I nearly didn't get the chance to play with Johnny Giles because some months earlier I had had another moan at the boss and he had agreed to let me go for the right price. The newspapers said that I could go for £30,000 which, they also said, was a ridiculously low price. That's not for me to say but it was purely academic anyway because nobody at all came in for me – at least nobody that I ever heard of! I never knew if I was unwanted or if it was another bit of the Revie kidology. Whatever it was, I'm very glad that I did not go because my partnership with Johnny Giles would probably never have happened and I now know what I would have missed.

'I have never known a quieter or more modest player than Johnny Giles. He always did his best to walk away from trouble even though he could look after himself more than adequately if he had to. He just didn't want to lower himself to the level of players who were capable of little more than kicking and punching. It has often been said that Johnny Giles was the most accurate passer of the ball in the game and I would not dispute that.'

The partnership began to work very quickly and, by Christmas 1963, Leeds had suffered only one League defeat. Then came their festive games against Sunderland, who had become their most fervent rivals in the race for promotion. At Elland Road on Boxing Day the result was a 1–1 draw. Two days later they met again at Roker Park and Sunderland won 2–1. It was a blow for Bremner and his Leeds mates, but they rallied to the cause and lost only one more game before the end of the season.

'We won promotion and in fact we finished as champions of the Second Division, two points clear of Sunderland. Our last home game of the season was against Plymouth and before the match we carried banners out onto the pitch. They read, "Thanks for your support". We played so badly afterwards that we only just managed to scrape a 1–1 draw with Plymouth, and we swore that we would never do such a thing again. While I was at Leeds we never did – it became something of a superstition. We made up for that poor performance against Plymouth by winning our final fixture, 2–0, away to Charlton Athletic. Alan Peacock scored both of our goals. Alan was not at Leeds for very long – but what a player! He had problems with his knees, otherwise I think he would have become one of the all-time greats. He was definitely great in the latter part of that season, scoring eight goals in the last fourteen games – which played a major part in our success and the return to the First Division.'

Promotion to the First Division was the start of a new era for Leeds United. Don Revie had clearly played it right. His choice of players and his choice of tactics had done the trick and the Leeds fans were more than happy. However, as the dustbins were filled with the empty champagne bottles, the question mark over whether or not Leeds could maintain their position in the top division was growing ever larger.

'I think there was already criticism of us growing outside Leeds. We had no worries about our ability to do well in the First Division. Our supporters had no doubts either and the local media boys were very confident too – but other people were saying that our style of play would not be successful against the big clubs. We were amazed by that because we always thought that we were one of the big clubs.

'The squad that won the Second Division championship was not just a bunch of no-hopers, or players who didn't really want to be playing in the top division. We were all very ambitious. Gary Sprake was our regular goalkeeper. He had started at the club as an apprentice and had made his debut in September 1962, when Tommy Younger was taken ill. Gary had an interesting debut because it was away to Swansea, which was near enough where he was born. He kept a clean sheet as we won 2–0 and he was hardly ever out of the side for the next ten years. He was as keen as anyone to be playing in the First Division.

'On the same day that Gary Sprake was making his debut, so was Paul Reaney at right-back and Norman Hunter at left-half. We had all been growing up together and, a year or so after we had become established in the side, Paul Madeley also came through. Albert Johanneson was dazzling everyone on the wing, Jim Storrie was banging in the goals along with Don Weston. Jack Charlton was being Jack Charlton, and with Ian Lawson, Willie Bell and, of course, Bobby Collins as the main squad members, we were looking forward to taking on the best of the First Division.'

There is no doubt that Revie's strategy was built around a rock-hard defence, energy efficiency and a will that was so strong that each player felt that he could run up Mount Everest with a pack on his back if the boss told him that it was going to earn a couple of points. Paul Madeley was just such a man and earned Billy Bremner's total admiration.

'Paul was our odd-job man – although that might sound a bit insulting. What I mean by that is that he would play anywhere and give the sort of performance that you would expect from someone who always played in that position. Paul Madeley is one of the most unassuming guys I have ever met and has always played down his own abilities. Being so versatile probably worked against him because he was one of those players who could cover for anyone. Before he became a first-team regular he was in and out of the side and played in nine different positions. I cannot praise him enough and I was delighted for him when he became an England international. He was what Leeds was all about; he could do anything for the club and his team-mates.'

Bremner also paid tribute to the contribution of Willie Bell.

'He was one of the older and more experienced players who had joined us from Queens Park. Willie had won two Scottish caps as an amateur, so he could do no wrong in my eyes. As it happened, he was the subject of a stroke of genius on the part of the boss, Don Revie, who turned him from being a competent half-back to a terrific full-back. Willie was always superbly fit and I doubt if there has ever been a tougher man in the game. He was a tremendous help to us youngsters making our way in the top flight.'

There was a cross-section of players in Revie's squad, the greatest strength being that so many of them were youngsters with their best years still to come. Since they were all from the same generation, the Leeds lads soon had a rapport both on and off the pitch. They were growing up and learning their trade together. They developed a playing understanding and a camaraderie that was rare. In a sense they put the 'United' into Leeds.

'We were all good pals,' said Billy. 'We went around together and we trusted each other. Successful teams thrive on a strong team spirit and sense of belonging. We certainly had that at Elland Road.'

Billy Bremner was a classic example of the Leeds spirit of

the time. By his own admission he was often in trouble with the authorities as the combination of youthful exuberance and an all-consuming passion for the game led him into situations which others might have avoided. However, there was no denying his ability and the Scotland selectors recognized that when they called him up for his first Under-23 cap.

It was a proud moment for Billy Bremner when he stepped out at St James' Park, Newcastle, on 5 February 1964 to take on the England Under-23 side.

'My first Scotland honour since I was a boy was a big moment in my career. It felt good to be wearing a Scotland shirt and I hoped that it would be a stepping stone to a full cap. It was a big ambition of mine to play for my country at senior level, even if it was only for one game. The Under-23 international game at Newcastle went against us. Fred Pickering scored a hat-trick for England and they won 3–2. We were disappointed because we really thought we had done enough at least to get a draw.

'My next game for the side was at the end of that season. The excitement of winning the Second Division with Leeds was still fresh in my mind when I was asked to put on the Scotland shirt again to face France. To add to the occasion we were playing away at Nantes. We came away with a creditable 2–0 victory. I don't think anyone expected us to pull off such a result. At best we were expected to grab a draw – but we had done much better than that, and coming, as it did, at the end of a good season, I was delighted with the result.'

Before the year was out, Bremner was called up once again for the Scotland Under-23 side – but by then Leeds were into the full swing of their first season back in Division One, and that is another story.

Bremner went on his summer holidays back in Scotland a happy and contented young man. He had left Raploch as a boy and returned as a man with a championship medal and Under-23 caps for his country. He was still Brock to his friends, but to

the rest of the world he was Billy Bremner, a professional footballer with skill, flair and a reputation – and he was still at the
beginning of his career.

4

LEEDS ON THE MARCH

Don Revie remained faithful to those who had helped Leeds United get back to the top flight. He made few changes to the squad, seeing that his nucleus of young players was growing up together and looking forward to taking on the best of English football.

'To me it meant that we were going to be playing against clubs like Manchester United, Arsenal, Tottenham, Liverpool and other teams who were household names and had been part of my soccer education as I was growing up,' said Billy. 'If I had not heard of Leeds before I joined the club, I had certainly heard of Sir Matt Busby and his great club. When the fixtures were announced we all gathered round to look at them like a bunch of schoolkids who were looking for their exam results. Our pre-season training was full of chat about who was going to be marking this player or that player. It was pretty pointless at that stage really, but we were just enjoying the speculation.

'Our first game was against Aston Villa at Villa Park and it was a typical opening day of the season, with the hot sun beating down on the pitch and the stadium packed with fans who were either wearing sunglasses or using one hand to shield their eyes from the sun. We were very keyed up before the game and we could hardly wait to get out there and get the game and the season started.

'When the whistle blew we were like greyhounds let out of the traps. The more experienced Villa players must have wondered what was going on. We launched attack after attack in the first quarter of an hour and ran Villa ragged. You can imagine how we felt when they opened the scoring. It was Phil Woosnam, the Welsh international, who calmly put Villa ahead while we were still chasing about the park. I couldn't believe it. I don't often panic but I distinctly remember a dark cloud of self-doubt passing over. "We're not going to be good enough," I thought.

'The boss couldn't wait to get us back in the dressing room. He didn't shout at us, but he told us quite firmly that we were to stop running about like a set of madmen and get down to playing calm football. That moment was another big step in our growing-up process. We went back out and played exactly as he had told us and Albert Johanneson equalized. We found that we were now matching Aston Villa pass for pass and gradually taking control of the game. Jack Charlton put us ahead and that is how it stayed until the end of the game. We had won 2–1, taken maximum points and had grown up a little, all in the space of one game.'

Having passed the opening test, Leeds had to show that their away win was no fluke. Bremner recalled these games with such ease that you would have thought that they had just been played.

'Our next game was at home to Liverpool. In many ways that was an even tougher test than the one we had just experienced. We now had to perform in front of our own supporters and give them the confidence that we were as good as anyone else in the First Division. Our win at Villa Park had definitely convinced us that we could get results, but we wanted more than that. Our sights were firmly set a lot higher than just survival. Liverpool were a magnificent side. Bill Shankly had transformed them into a very special outfit and we knew they were coming to Elland Road intent on securing maximum points. We had also been made aware that a part of Shankly's psychology was to convince his players that they were playing against a bunch of nobodies, half of whom were limping. He was a canny guy and a brilliant manager and everyone respected him tremendously, but we also rated our own manager and we knew that he would have us prepared to take on and beat anybody.

'Liverpool came to Elland Road as reigning champions. Don Revie told us to go out and prove that we were a match, and more, for them. His words inspired us and put us in exactly the right frame of mind for the task ahead. It was quite a task, of course, but we settled quickly and played the way we had performed in the second half against Villa. Liverpool were excellent – as good as we had expected – but we were not going to pay them too much respect and I think they were uneasy long before we were because the unflappable Ron Yeats scored our first goal for us. I pulled his leg about that later. As a fellow Scot I got away with it. He opened the floodgates with that own goal because Don Weston, Johnny Giles and I each followed it up with a goal and we ran out 4–2 winners. Our supporters certainly celebrated after that!'

They were celebrating again a few days later, when Wolves were also beaten at Elland Road. Three games played and three victories. Suddenly, Leeds were a team to be taken seriously.

'We were on a bit of a high at that time. We were starting to believe that we were potential champions. It did not last long because the manager was not only good at encouraging us, he was also good at keeping our feet on the ground. He reminded us that pride comes before a fall – and he was right.'

The tumble came in the fourth game of the season when Leeds played their return fixture against Liverpool. They were in no mood to be beaten twice by the newly promoted Leeds side and ran out 2–1 winners at Anfield, but not before Bobby Collins had kept Leeds in the frame with a goal and there had been various near misses. After that match there was another away trip a few days later, this time to Sunderland.

'The result we got there was one of the most pleasing of the season for me. Having been promoted together, the rivalry between the two clubs had become even more intense. There was almost a hate campaign running between the two clubs and, when we went two goals ahead in the game, thanks to Jim Storrie and Willie Bell, we became a little too cocky. Sunderland had not given up by any means and from 2–0 ahead we went to 3–2 behind with just ten minutes left. Albert Johanneson had not given up either and he grabbed us an equalizer. In some ways we were a little lucky to come away with a point but, on the whole, the reason I found it so satisfying was that we had the chance to compare ourselves with the other team who had been promoted that year, and I firmly believe that we had made more progress and much faster than they had.

'Mentioning Albert Johanneson, I would like to say what an excellent player he was. He was frightening on the wing and used to turn defenders inside out. He was fast, clever with the footwork, very accurate with crosses, and had a terrific shot. I always thought that he did not get a fair deal from the media because he was black. They were forever on about him being the first black player to do this, or the first black player to do that. They completely overlooked the fact that he was a terrific player and deserved recognition as a human being and a professional footballer.'

Only two days after the Sunderland game Leeds were at Blackpool playing their third First Division away match in a week. There was an even greater setback when they lost 4–0.

'We came up against Alan Ball. That day at Bloomfield Road he was fantastic. We never seemed to see which way he had gone and I came off the field feeling utterly choked and determined to do better when we met again at Elland Road. That day came about a fortnight later, but there had been a bit of drama in between. We had got back to winning ways with a 3–2 win at home to Leicester – but behind the scenes we had heard some devastating news – Don Revie was leaving to become manager of Sunderland.

'It was very difficult to come to terms with that. It meant a return to his roots for Revie but, to the rest of us, it meant that he was leaving us and joining our rivals. Perhaps most people might have thought that we looked upon him as a traitor – but we didn't at all. He had made us and, even if he did leave, we could never thank him enough for what he had done for us as individuals and as a team. We were determined that we should win his farewell game, and win it well as a gift to him to show him what he had created.

'Blackpool had no answer for us as we stormed into action. We won 3–0 with Bobby Collins scoring two and Norman Hunter getting one. I disgraced myself by missing two penalties, but a 3–0 victory was pretty good and we were worth it. Then came the news that the boss was not leaving after all. The newspapers had turned a vague possibility into an actual event and we had all swallowed it. He called all the players together and told us to forget about any idea that he might be going somewhere. He had started a job at Leeds and he was going to see it through. We were delighted to hear it, of course. Some time later he was linked with a vacancy at Manchester United, but this time we didn't fall for it and, once again, Don Revie stayed with us.'

Leeds were still in the process of learning about life in the First Division and, as the team grew in stature, so did its individual players.

'For us youngsters it was a really fascinating season because we were coming up against men whom we only knew by reputation. Players like Johnny Haynes, Jimmy Greaves and so on were opposing us every week. The boss warned us against Jimmy Greaves. He told us that we must not give him any room in which to work. We did pretty well too, but even so he managed to sneak in and get a goal against us at Elland Road when we were at home to Tottenham. The good thing is that we won 3–1, and I remember that Rod Belfitt scored his first League goal for us in only his second League match. I think the win over Tottenham came just a few days after we had been knocked out of the League Cup by Aston Villa. Up to then the League Cup had not been one of our strong points and we usually made an early exit.'

Leeds saw another side of the First Division in November 1964 when they were away to Everton in a game that went

35

down in history. Leeds won 1–0, but the result tells nothing of the story of the game which turned into a mini-war.

'The tackles were going in as if it was a matter of life and death and tempers, already frayed at the start, were completely lost as the game wore on. There were professional footballers out there who had completely forgotten what they were there for. The ball was actually getting in the way of revenge missions. To regain control of the situation, the referee called a halt to the game and took us all off to cool down for ten minutes before completing the match. We had been branded "the dirtiest team in the League" and that game did not do anything to help us shed that tag. When we played the return game at Elland Road, Everton wanted revenge for the 1–0 defeat – and for the fact that we had also knocked them out of the FA Cup. To their credit, they wanted revenge by playing football and we were quite happy to play it the same way. It must have been a very disappointing afternoon for the army of press photographers who had made the pilgrimage to Elland Road in the hope of taking pictures of another bloody battle between the two clubs.'

That was not the only incident lodged in Billy's memory of that first season back in Division One.

'When we went to Old Trafford for the first time we lost our cool once again – but not with the opposition. We were leading with a goal from Bobby Collins and we could sense victory. Manchester United could not break us down. We were far too disciplined in defence and they could not find a way through. Then, with eight minutes to go, the fog that had been swirling around the ground suddenly became much worse and the referee halted the game. We went absolutely crazy and told him that he couldn't possibly abandon the game, that we could still see from the halfway line, that the spectators wouldn't mind because they had already seen the best part of the game, and so on and so on. The poor man could not get a word in. A few of us were still young and impetuous in those days and we had a bit of a chip on our shoulders too. Referees were authority and we kicked against that at every opportunity – even if we were harming ourselves by doing it. When the referee finally got to have his say he explained that the fog had been made worse by a passing steam train and that he was only waiting for a couple of minutes for the smoke to clear. He was as good as his word and about four minutes later we returned to the game and played out the last eight minutes with no further goals.'

A few days before that game, Bremner had won his third Scotland Under-23 cap when he lined up against Wales at Kilmarnock. Scotland won 3–0 and he scored in a performance which had the Scottish press demanding his call-up to the senior side. They were soon to have their way, but not just yet.

Bremner missed just two matches that season as Leeds tore into the opposition time after time. At one stage they were at the top of the League. Their championship dreams were becoming a real possibility as they continued on a run that the rest of the First Division clubs found devastating. Criticism of the Leeds style became more and more frequent. Victory was more important than style, or so it seemed. In fact, Leeds were very stylish, but they were tough too, and any beaten manager preferred to point to the hard side of the Leeds character than admit that his side had been outplayed.

The games that Billy Bremner missed were a torture to him. His running wars with referees had earned him a suspension and he hated it.

'It was only then that I found out what the boss and his assistants go through every week as they sit on the touchline watching us try to take the points. I sat there and fidgeted while we beat West Brom 2–1 in a game in which they were definitely the better side but we happened to get the goals. I don't know how many times my heart stopped beating. The following game was the return against Manchester United and once again I had to sit there and watch. The Manchester lads beat us and I think that put paid to our hopes of the championship. We only had four games left. We lost to Sheffield Wednesday at Hillsborough and then beat them at home the next day. We played Sheffield United and beat them, but then came crunch

37

time. Manchester United had near enough wrapped up the championship but there was still an outside chance that we might pull off something. However, we had also been progressing in the FA Cup and, the very week that we were due to play against Liverpool in the final at Wembley, we were told that we must also fulfil our League fixtures. It could not wait until after the Cup Final, so we had to go to Birmingham City.

'That last game was a drama all of its own. The boss told us to take it easy because of the Cup Final and we took him at his word. We went 3–0 down. Then I suddenly saw him on the touchline waving his arms about. You don't really hear what people are saying to you from off the pitch, but we got the message that he wanted us to get back into the game. We started to put the foot on the accelerator and pulled one back when Johnny Giles scored from a penalty. Jack Charlton made it 3–2, and then Paul Reaney went on a run and scored a lovely goal to make it 3–3. For the last few minutes, the Birmingham goal area had twenty-one players camped in it. If we could get one more goal we would be champions. We didn't, and then the news came through that Manchester United had grabbed a late winner at Arsenal and their 1–0 victory gave them the championship on goal average.'

As mentioned elsewhere, Leeds were also pipped for the FA Cup, and what might have been one of the most sensational doubles of all time, by a team that had only just come into the top division, turned out to be a story of what might have been.

'We were devastated at not winning anything. Yet it had been a fantastic season. Nobody had expected us to come close to winning anything at all, let alone two of the toughest competitions in world football. For me it was a great season. I had learned so much. I had been capped again by the Under-23 side in February, when we drew 0–0 with England at Aberdeen – and I had been called up to the senior squad. All that had come about because no one had taken me seriously when I asked to leave Leeds. I was so grateful that they hadn't.'

Bremner once took me through a typical week's work at Leeds United.

'It varied quite a bit really because of the midweek commitments which became more and more as time went by because of the increased competitions. On what we might call a "normal" week, we usually turned up in our cars just before 10 a.m. Even that used to have some people cribbing.

'In the old days, players always lived near the ground and were able to walk to the club for training. It was a different world then, though, and that walk probably did them more good than it would have done in my day because there were no techniques that were taxing enough. You didn't need the extra exercise of a twenty-minute walk before you started. Some of today's players will tell you that they do not play golf in the season because it is too tiring. That probably sounds a bit far-fetched, but the fact is that your legs are working all the time when you are a professional player and the last thing that you need is even more work for them – especially at a time when you are supposed to be relaxing. When I was a player, the same thing applied. I have always enjoyed a game of golf, but you have to be sensible and play only when you are able. Having said that, golf was always popular among the Leeds players and still is, I believe. A group of us used to play regularly and, before the season started, we used to have our own club championship with a big trophy at stake. Johnny Giles, Norman Hunter and Mick Jones were our golfing stars, and they were quite a match for each other while the rest of us were usually also-rans.

'Few of our players lived near the ground. Most lived on the outskirts of Leeds and just could not walk to work. We liked to live outside the main city because it meant some peace for our families and ourselves when we had time off. So, we would turn up at Elland Road in our flash cars, which also used to raise a few eyebrows. A lot of the older generation of fans had not got used to the new era of higher wages for players, and I think some were a little resentful of the fact that we were able to afford a more luxurious lifestyle than their previous heroes. It wasn't our fault. It was just that we happened to be born when we were. I don't moan about the wages that players get now. Well, I do sometimes – but only when I see a player who doesn't really deserve it.

'The morning discussion at Leeds was usually about the sports news we had read in the morning papers, or about horse racing or the previous night's television. Once we were all in the dressing room we would get changed while carrying on our conversations. Les Cocker used to come and get us when he was ready to start and then we would go out and warm up for about twenty minutes. That would involve stretching exercises to get the muscles ready for the real action to follow.

'Once warmed up we would probably then go for circuit training. This was a wide variety of exercises. Some would involve weightlifting, while others would be to do with ball control. The exercises were varied so that we didn't know exactly what we would be doing next. It kept us mentally alert and stopped us from getting bored or complacent.

'Next came five-a-side games. Don't think that these were just a bit of fun. They were always highly competitive and played under match conditions. One of the things that made them so competitive was that we used to take a secret ballot on which player had put in the worst performance and whoever was elected had to wear a yellow jersey with an outsize "wooden spoon" on the back. Nobody wanted to have to wear that and so the tackles were always going in strong and there was always an extra edge to the game.

'After the game we were usually pretty exhausted, but that was not the end of training as we still had our running to do – sprints and jogs which helped to build up our stamina. By the time we had done all that we were ready to have a bath and a cup of tea. The jokes and jibing that went on then were as much because of the relief at having finished as it was a demonstration of the team spirit which unified us so much.

'It would be late lunchtime when we returned home and the rest of the time was ours – although most of us were in the habit of getting some rest each afternoon. Of course, it would not be like that on match day and it was also varied from day to day. Our coaches worked hard at providing us with different training regimes each day to keep us on our toes.

'If there was a midweek match, we would have a light training session in the morning, and then relax, often going to sleep in the afternoon to conserve energy. If the game was away from home, we would quite often have travelled there the day before, but there was not much chance of sight-seeing or shopping as we were always encouraged to rest as much as possible when we were not training.

'For Saturday games at home, we always left our families behind on the Friday. We would train in the morning, go home for a while, and then return to the call around tea time. A coach would then take us to a hotel in the Yorkshire Dales where we could not be disturbed. That practice actually changed while I was at Leeds because of all the European games. We found that we were spending just too much time away from our families and so the policy of going away before a home game was altered. We still went away on Friday nights before important games, but we stayed at our own homes for ordinary fixtures. That was basically how a week went by when I was a player with Leeds. Perhaps it sounds easy, but you have to make a lot of sacrifices for your profession. You don't see anywhere near as much of your family as you would really like. You stand a better chance when your playing career is over, but if you become a coach or a manager then you are still on the treadmill.

'As Leeds players we were encouraged to represent the club as well, and as much as possible. That meant attending functions where the public could meet us and hopefully become supporters. Sometimes it would be at a prize-giving, or an annual dance, or even walking round a local factory. Most of us enjoyed it, but it did still mean that the time that was actually our own became more and more limited. Fortunately, most girlfriends become used to their men being away for a lot of the time and, if those same girlfriends eventually become wives, they have already accepted what life is going to be like married to a footballer – at least while their other half is still playing.

'At Elland Road we had a couple of characters who went together like ham and eggs. Their names were Owen and Cocker. Syd Owen was the manager of Luton at one time, already having served them as a player, won the "Footballer of the Year" award with them, and made his final appearance with them in an FA Cup Final at Wembley. Les Cocker had been around a bit. He was a centre-forward who could score goals. He had been with the unfashionable clubs like Stockport County and the defunct Accrington Stanley. He had no special frills, he was just a fellow who really knew what his job was. When they came together at Elland Road, they made a formidable combination.

'When Syd was still manager at Luton he was looking for a trainer. Les Cocker applied for the job and got it. Syd Owen had never met him before but he knew that Les was the man for him. When Syd finally joined Leeds he persuaded Les to come as well, and there they stuck, despite offers of jobs elsewhere. These two characters did much more than train the lads in their care. They spent hours in analysing a youngster's abilities, finding out how to improve on his strong points, and even how to eradicate or at least remedy his weaknesses. And believe me, every player has weaknesses which he does his best to conceal from other people. That means that the Owens and Cockers of this world must be prepared to spend countless hours giving individual attention to each youngster on the club's staff.

'Perhaps the point is made clearer when I tell you that I still shudder when I think of all the hours of hard graft that I spent under those two taskmasters. They made me lose buckets of sweat – but everything that they told me was for my own good, and any improvement that I ever made was thanks to their constant attention to detail.

'All the time that I was at Leeds it was drilled into me that a footballer is not only in the game when the ball is at his feet. Owen and Cocker analysed players and they affirmed that, out of the ninety minutes of the game, a player who retains possession the longest still only has the ball for three minutes. Syd and Les made it clear to all of us at Elland Road that they expected us lads to work hardest when we hadn't got the ball at our feet. We discovered through these two great characters that whether Leeds were attacking or defending, everyone was expected to play his part for the other eighty-seven minutes of the game, not just the three already mentioned. These men didn't just tell us about it, they showed us how to achieve it. We had a happy ship at Leeds United, and I think that played a major part in our success.'

When Billy reflected on those days it was almost as if he was still there. It was a remarkable example of how age is merely a shell. It is the fruit inside that really lives, even when the outer shell has worn a little.

5

THE BATTLE FOR THE FA CUP

Billy Bremner was as passionate about winning the FA Cup as any Englishman. It is sometimes assumed, quite mistakenly, that if a footballer is not born in England, the FA Cup can never mean quite the same to him as to a player who is. In Billy's case that was definitely far from the truth. He was a student of the game and he had read the stories of Wembley Cup Finals – and of finals from even before that great stadium became the spiritual home of the world's most famous cup competition. He was well aware of the heroics of Scots in past English Cup Finals – men like Jackie Mudie, Matt Busby and Alex James. He was also well aware of the great displays by Scottish teams of yesterday at Wembley, the celebrated 'Wembley Wizards' among them.

As a Scotsman, his greatest love was the annual Scottish Cup Final, and long after his retirement he still liked to attend the game as often as he could but, while he was playing in England, he knew that he had the chance to fly the flag for Scotland in the English showpiece of the year. There was an added incentive, too. Leeds United had never appeared in the FA Cup Final at any time in the club's long history. Now, there was a challenge.

'I was aware that the club had never achieved much in the FA Cup and I remember thinking how I would love to change all that,' he said. He certainly did change the situation, too, but it took much longer than he had hoped and there were a lot of disappointments before that great day of triumph.

44

Billy's very first game in the FA Cup was on 7 January 1961, in the third round at Bramall Lane, home of Sheffield United. Sporting the No. 10 shirt, which had mostly been worn by Irish international Noel Peyton that season, Bremner gave a very lively performance but was unable to prevent his side from going down 2–0.

'I had a few things to say when we were back in the dressing room,' Billy recalled. 'I don't know why they took it really. I was just an eighteen-year-old lad with too much to say. They must all have been tuned into their own thoughts while I was having my moan.'

A couple of months after that defeat, Don Revie became manager and there was a new air of optimism. However, the next FA Cup campaign lasted little longer than the previous one. Derby County provided the opposition and won the third-round tie after a replay. A 2–2 draw in the first game was followed by a 3–1 success for Derby in the replay at the Baseball Ground. Bremner wore the No. 7 shirt in both games.

In the following season, the FA Cup campaign proved to be even more frustrating. Leeds reached the fifth round before making their exit as the result of a convincing 3–0 defeat at the hands of Nottingham Forest. There was little pleasure for Bremner in Leeds United's improvement as he missed each of the three games because of injury.

There was a major breakthrough in the 1963/64 season. It wasn't that Leeds fared any better than before – they were eliminated in the fourth round by Everton after a replay at Goodison – but in the third round they had defeated Cardiff 1–0 away from home, and guess who scored the goal?

'I remember that goal,' said Billy. 'It wasn't just the goal itself but the fact that it was me who scored it and that it had got us through to the next round. I had been trying for four years to score a goal in the FA Cup and that one was a major milestone for me.'

More than a year passed before he was able to repeat the performance. A 3–0 home win over Southport provided a safe passage to the fourth round and it seemed almost a case of déjà vu as Leeds came out of the hat alongside Everton. Once again the fourth-round tie was to be played at home, and once again the score was 1–1. This time, however, Leeds were better prepared for the replay and it was Everton who emerged as the beaten side while Leeds travelled home with the cheers of their fans still ringing in their ears. They had triumphed 2–1. A 2–0 win over Shrewsbury meant that Leeds were in the quarter-finals and looking very good indeed. Crystal Palace were next in line and stood between Leeds United and their first-ever FA Cup semi-final.

'We were really keyed up and ready to go,' said Billy. 'We had prepared well and we were on an unbeaten run. Then the weather took a hand in it and the game was frozen off. The pitch was like granite and, having mentally peaked for the tie, we were forced to wait for a few more days. That can be very frustrating for players when all the preparations for a particular game have been made and something as unexpected as that happens. Anyway, we played a few days later and we won 3–0 so there were no complaints from us. The referee had been right to postpone the game and the weather always has the last word.'

Leeds were now in unknown territory. Their semi-final opponents were Manchester United whom they had already beaten once in the League a few months previously. Bobby Collins was proving to be the great inspiration for the side while Billy Bremner was playing like a man inspired. He was indefatigable and his presence seemed to be growing with every game.

'That was a tough semi-final, as you would expect. I don't think it was a great game for the supporters at Hillsborough. It finished at 0–0 and we never really looked like breaking the deadlock. It was much the same when we played again at Nottingham a few days later, but we managed to get a late goal.'

Bremner's terse match report did not mention that the

winning goal came in the eighty-eighth minute and that it was his head which had sent the ball into the net. Typically, he had refused to settle even for extra-time.

There were great celebrations in the city of Leeds and a tremendous build-up of excitement began as the FA Cup Final drew near.

In the League, Leeds United had been pipped at the post for the title by Manchester United. That disappointment meant that it was now the FA Cup or nothing for Leeds. Sadly it was nothing – nothing but the tears of disappointment as Liverpool won the game 2–1 and took home the trophy.

After Roger Hunt had scored, putting Liverpool into the lead, Bremner was pushed up front in a do-or-die attempt to get an equalizer. He scored and the ninety minutes finished at 1–1. The game then moved into extra-time.

'I still believe that if I had gone back in defence after scoring the equalizer,' said Billy, 'we could have settled for a replay at Maine Road on the following Wednesday.'

It is very easy to be wise after the event, and Billy could just as possibly have scored another goal by staying up front. As it happened it was Liverpool who scored again – this time through Ian St John – during that period of extra-time. The season ended for Leeds with Bremner very much aware that two honours had been snatched away from them in the space of a week.

'We were devastated – there's no other way of putting it. The after-match banquet was more like a wake. It wasn't so much that we had lost but that we all felt that we hadn't played as well as we could. I suppose that nerves played a part to some extent. But it didn't alter matters, knowing that we had come within an ace of winning one of the game's major honours and that, because we hadn't raised our game accordingly, we had faltered at the final hurdle.

'Everyone tried to put on a brave face, and there were smiles and the odd joke, but we were all working at it to try to give each other a lift. Inside we were all totally depressed. The boss was doing his best, telling us that we'd had a good season and that our day would come. I'm sure that he was feeling just as bad as we were inside.'

The following season optimism was high as Leeds sailed through their first FA Cup tie, a third-round 6–0 cruise at home to Bury. Then came the fourth-round clash with a side that was to prove to be a thorn in the side of both Bremner and Leeds United – Chelsea. Leeds' Cup hopes were blown apart by a 1–0 defeat at Stamford Bridge. In the future Chelsea were to come back and again to end Leeds' hopes of an historic success.

'They became a bit of a bogey team in the FA Cup. They were a good side and they had turned into a good FA Cup side. They didn't give much away and they were quick to take advantage of any stray chances. They knocked us out in the 1965/66 season, 1–0 – and then they did the same thing in the semi-final the next season at Villa Park. I think they only got one real chance and that was it.'

It wasn't quite it, though. The game had been controversial since United had been denied a late equalizer.

'We had already had one perfectly good goal disallowed when I slipped the ball to Terry Cooper and he smacked it in. The referee said he was offside but there was no way that he was. We were furious but we still had six or seven minutes left and we had to concentrate on the job. Then, right at the end of it, we got a free kick on the edge of their box. Johnny Giles slipped it to Peter Lorimer and the next thing it was in the back of the net. We all leaped in the air but then we realized that something was wrong. The referee disallowed the goal and ordered the kick to be retaken because the Chelsea players had not been ten yards from the ball. He should have given us the advantage and we all told him so – and a few other things as well. We could not believe it. We had to take the kick again but this time Chelsea cleared it. There is no doubt in my mind that we were robbed. No argument with the Chelsea goal but to be denied our equalizer was a travesty.'

When the next FA Cup campaign started, Leeds were at

home to Swansea and, to be honest, they struggled to get a 2–1 win over their spirited Welsh visitors. The reward was a fourth-round match at non-League Sutton which Leeds won comfortably, 6–0.

'Those are difficult matches,' remarked Billy. 'The grounds and the pitches are all in favour of the non-League side and the bigger club is on a hiding into nothing. If you win well it is no more than you should have done, if you don't then you are put up against a wall and shot by the press. Allan Clarke scored four and Peter Lorimer got a couple and we were happy with that.'

Mansfield were the next victims, followed by Swindon – and then came the semi-final and another meeting with Manchester United. Once again Billy Bremner proved to be the man who settled the fate of both clubs.

'This was another of those games you can never forget. We met at Hillsborough and once again we were back on the FA Cup treadmill with a 0–0 draw. The season was due to finish early in 1970 because of the World Cup tournament that was to follow, so the last thing that anyone needed was a fixture pile-up. Nine days after the first game we met again at Villa Park. We had already played United twice in the League and both games had ended at 2–2, so it seemed that our Cup matches were likely to end in stalemate too.

'I was particularly keen to get a result from the replay because in between times I had been named as "Footballer of the Year". It was a tremendous honour and meant a lot to me. The previous year I had been runner-up to David Mackay and Tony Book who had jointly won this great award. I never expected to do any better than that so when I heard that I was "Footballer of the Year" I was really taken aback. I had worked hard at trying to keep out of trouble on the pitch and I thought that perhaps I was being recognized for that as much as for any football ability.

'Despite the best efforts of both sides, the Villa Park replay ended at 0–0 just like our first game. Extra-time had made no difference and we had to play again, this time at Bolton's

Burnden Park. I think that both sides knew that there would probably be only one goal between us and we went at it hammer and tongs to be the first to score. After almost ten minutes we finally broke the deadlock. A high ball went to Allan Clarke, he nodded it down and it hit Mick Jones on the legs and rebounded away from the United goal and straight to me. I didn't hesitate and just fired it in. It flew about thirty-five yards and smashed into the net. It was a fantastic feeling.

'There was still most of the game to go so we had to keep our discipline. United tried everything but, at the end of it, our one goal proved to be the decider and we were on our way back to Wembley again. The only problem was that we had to play against Chelsea who had proved to be such a pain to us in Cup games.

'They were no different in the final at Wembley. We had had a few poor results in the run-up to the FA Cup Final, and we were a bit depressed until just a few days before the game. Then the buzz began to go through us and we were determined that, win or lose, we would show everyone that we could play real football. Somehow we had earned a reputation of being a dirty side and defensive to the extreme. That was never true. We were a hard side but we didn't go around kicking people, as some seemed to think.

'The actual game went into the history books because we played the full ninety minutes and a half-hour of extra-time without getting a result. A replay was needed for the first time in fifty-eight years, but it had not been a drab match. Both sides were applauded off the pitch and the newspapers called it one of the best Cup Finals of all time – gruelling but entertaining. I wonder if they realized just how gruelling it had been. We were all absolutely shattered when we came off the pitch. The pitch itself had been in a terrible condition because of all the rain we had had. There had been tons of sand put on it and at times you found yourself ankle-deep in water, mud and sand. Try running on that, let alone passing the ball!

'The game was about twenty minutes old when we scored. Jack Charlton headed down from a corner and the Chelsea defenders on the goal-line completely missed the ball. It rolled over the line and we were ahead. It didn't last long because, just before half-time, Peter Houseman sent in a low shot which Gary Sprake seemed to have covered – but the ball skidded under him somehow and into the net. In the second half it was an end-to-end game in which I think we just about had the edge. We hit their bar and went close several times, but it was not until about seven minutes before the end that we went ahead again. Mick Jones saw a chance and sent the ball low into the corner of the net.

'I think everyone thought that was it but, to our despair, Chelsea came back again and Ian Hutchinson headed home from a free kick with only a minute to go. We were devastated. Throughout extra-time the game was played at the same pace, but there were no more goals. There could be no Cup presentation but we all went up to meet Princess Margaret, who said: "I'm sorry you haven't got the Cup yet!" I don't know if she said the same thing to Chelsea but it certainly gave me something to think about ... Princess Margaret – a Leeds fan?

'We replayed at Old Trafford and continued where we had left off. I don't think that any Chelsea fan would dispute that we had most of the play – but it's goals that count. We were not far from half-time when Allan Clarke went on a run. He beat three players and then slipped it to Mick Jones who slotted it straight into the net. It was a great goal, a classic, and typical of the partnership that Allan and Mick had formed. We kept our heads and battled away for the rest of the game but, with less than a quarter of an hour left, Chelsea gathered strength and gave the game what I think was there last big effort. It worked for them as Charlie Cooke sent the ball into the middle for Peter Osgood to dive and head home. We were all square again and it stayed that way until the whistle ended the game. Extra-time was necessary again.

'We were almost halfway through it when our world

51

turned upside down. Jack Charlton went up to head clear but the ball spun off him and straight to David Webb who was almost on our goal-line. He had a simple task of nodding it over the line and, for the first time, Chelsea were ahead. We pounded their goal after that but they stood firm and, when the game ended, we were all flat on the floor. It wasn't just that we were totally exhausted, but that we were also defeated. We had nothing to show for our season despite being runners-up in the two major domestic competitions and semi-finalists in the European Cup.

'As you can imagine, our dressing room was the most miserable place on earth after that game. Nobody wanted to look at their medals. It was the boss who brought us back to life again. He didn't say much but his well-chosen words gave us something to think about. He simply said: "We've got to start all over again. We've done it before and we can do it again." Somehow that changed our focus from what had just happened to what we were going to make happen in the future.'

What a difference a season makes. In the 1970/71 season, Leeds began their road to Wembley with a third-round victory over Rotherham after a replay. Then came an emphatic 4–0 victory over Swindon, the reward for which was a fifth-round tie at Colchester – which proved to be a game that the television companies love to recall every year. The unthinkable happened!

'I missed this game and we had several injury worries. Colchester had Ray Crawford upfront. He was getting on a bit but he knew his way around the park and shed about ten years as Colchester went into a 3–0 lead. Norman Hunter and Johnny Giles pulled two goals back, but Colchester defended superbly and held on to win 3–2. The newspapers had a field day. The mighty Leeds United had fallen. I felt sick!'

It seemed that Leeds were destined never to win the FA Cup, but of course that was not the case. In fact, it was the very next season of 1971/72 that the great dream finally came true.

The road to Wembley had taken an unusual route. Bristol Rovers had been first to go, followed by Liverpool, after a replay in which two Allan Clarke goals proved decisive. A win at Cardiff City earned a home quarter-final tie against Tottenham and then, once they were dispatched, Birmingham City provided the obstacle in the semi-final at Hillsborough. Mick Jones scored two and Peter Lorimer the other in a 3–0 win and, once again, Wembley beckoned. The potential omen of playing another London club in the final was ignored – Leeds were determined to win this one and Arsenal were not going to stop them.

'We remembered what had happened on our previous visits to Wembley for the FA Cup Final and, while we did not dwell on those times, they certainly helped to make us all the more determined and single-minded. Arsenal were a tough side. They had won the Cup the year before and they were keen to hold on to it and so the game was definitely not going to be a picnic. As it happened, this was the Centenary Final and the FA had decided to have some special events before the game. We were not involved in that, but I believe it was all a bit of a shambles which did not surprise me. The only professional point was when Tommy Steele led some singing.

'The actual game surprised us. We were expecting Arsenal to have a go, but they played a really negative game. It seemed as if they were just trying to contain us. We tried to play flowing football but Arsenal did their best to destroy everything. There was a strange atmosphere in the game as well. Within the first minute Bob McNab made sure that the game went down in history when he was booked for a foul on Peter Lorimer. I think he was the first player ever to get booked in an FA Cup Final. Norman Hunter also got booked later for a foul. Charlie George joined Bob McNab in the Arsenal bookings list and we had another man booked too – me! I didn't foul anyone. I just tried to discuss matters with the referee, that's all. Perhaps I should have chosen my words more carefully, but whatever, I impressed him enough for him to make a note of my name.

'Arsenal had their moments and they could have been two goals ahead by half-time. David Harvey pulled off a fantastic save and Paul Reaney cleared off the line. Not that we didn't go close. Allan Clarke headed against the crossbar and, in the second half, Peter Lorimer hit the post. Nobody knew until after the game that Johnny Giles had played throughout with an injury and had been given a pain-killing jab before the match.

'The winner came after about ten minutes of the second half. It was that Jones–Clarke partnership again. Mick Jones got the ball on the right and went past McNab before sending over a beautiful cross that fooled the Arsenal defence. I think they were expecting something high in the air, but Allan Clarke knew what he was about and stooped to meet it with his head and put it into the right-hand corner of their net. It was a beauty.

'We kept battling for another and we virtually ran the second half. We almost made it 2–0 just before the end when Mick Jones broke through – it took a very brave dive at his feet by the Arsenal goalkeeper, Geoff Barnett, to save it. The collision between the two left Mick in a heap on the ground and he was still there when the final whistle blew. Les Cocker ran over to him with the doctor and they could see that it was going to be a stretcher job. He was in terrible pain with his arm. We delayed going up to collect the trophy for as long as possible, hoping that he would be all right to collect his medal. Unfortunately he wasn't, and so the rest of us eventually climbed those stairs to meet Her Majesty the Queen. I wiped my hands on my shirt and she gave me a lovely smile. I think she said: "Very well done! You have earned it," but you don't really take it all in that well when you've got thousands of people just waiting for you to lift the trophy in the air.

'It was a very proud moment when I raised the FA Cup above my head. No other Leeds captain had done that and to me it represented a lot of hard work by everyone connected with our club, including our brilliant supporters. I felt like saying, "Here it is! You've all won it!" Norman Hunter collected Mick Jones's medal and we could see that he was still being attended to. It was difficult to know whether to take the trophy to him or to the supporters. The Wembley security made up our minds for us by showing us the way for the lap of honour. However, we delayed it because Mick was back on his feet. He was desperate to go up and meet the Queen and Norman Hunter went over and helped him up the steps. The whole of Wembley rose to him. It was a fantastic sight to see him, with his dislocated elbow heavily strapped and being assisted by Norman, going slowly up those steps to meet the Queen. I'll never forget that. We waited until he had come down again before we went on our lap of honour. Mick was stretchered away to hospital, but at least he had fulfilled his ambition.'

The following season, Leeds returned to Wembley for the FA Cup Final of 1973, but the story was very different. On the way they had beaten Norwich in the third round. It took two replays to pull them apart, Leeds winning the third game 5–0. Plymouth, West Brom and Derby provided the next obstacles and Leeds passed through all of them – although they did not look as comfortable as FA Cup holders might. It was Bremner himself who settled the semi-final against Wolves at Maine Road. His goal was the only one of the tie and Leeds were through to the Wembley showpiece again for the third time in four years.

'It turned out to be a nightmare. Sunderland were in the Second Division but they had played well to get to the final with attacking football that had beaten Arsenal in the semi-final, so we knew that they were not going to be easy – even though everyone kept telling us that we were favourites by a mile.

'We set about the task with our usual style but Sunderland were determined not to let us settle. They chased and chased and chased. They concentrated on breaking up the partnership between Mick Jones and Allan Clarke and they were successful. Their goalkeeper, Jimmy Montgomery, was in brilliant form and has gone down in football history for one fantastic double-save he pulled off when Trevor Cherry and Peter Lorimer both looked certain to score. He pushed away Trevor's header and then somehow got to Peter's attempt from the rebound. I think we knew then that we were never going to score. Ian Porterfield had put them ahead after half an hour but that had not worried us because we had been confident of scoring a goal or two ourselves. When Montgomery saved like that we didn't stop trying, but I think we all felt that it was not going to be our day. When the final whistle went we were all totally fed up, but I think we were also a bit relieved that it was all over.'

Leeds have not reached the FA Cup Final since 1973. Bristol City put them out in the fifth round the following year, and Ipswich put paid to their chances in the 1974/75 season, their sixth-round tie going to four games before it was decided.

'We were sick of the sight of Ipswich that year. We drew 0–0 at their place in a League match earlier in that season. Then we drew 0–0 there again in our first Cup game. The replay at Elland Road went to extra-time and ended at 1–1. We had a second replay at Leicester and that ended 0–0 after extra-time, and then we played again at Leicester two days later and they finished up as 3–2 winners. A few weeks later we had to play them in the League again and beat them 2–1 at home. However, we had seen enough of them that season.'

Billy Bremner's very last FA Cup tie as a Leeds United player was in the fourth round of the 1975/76 competition when his team lost 0–1 at home to Crystal Palace. It was not quite the end of his FA Cup playing career as he competed in the third round for Hull City in both of the following two seasons – going out to Port Vale in the first season and Leicester in the second. Later, of course, he was involved in the competition as a manager, but it was his playing experience that meant the most to him.

'The FA Cup is all about making history,' he reflected. 'I have been in some historic matches both in the earlier rounds and in the final itself. I certainly know what it is like to have to go to your supporters and thank them for their backing when you have lost, and I have also been to those same supporters and shown them the trophy. That's what it is all about really – days when you can cry your eyes out and days when you can walk on air. There is nothing to compare.'

6

CHAMPIONS

When the 1965/66 season began, Leeds were even more anxious to get their hands on a trophy. They had four chances because, in addition to the three domestic competitions, the club was in Europe for the first time – competing in what was then the Inter-Cities Fairs Cup. The extra challenge might have been a wolf in sheep's clothing as it may well have robbed the club of the League championship.

Leeds began the season well enough with a victory over rivals Sunderland at Elland Road, followed by a 2–0 win at Aston Villa. A defeat at West Ham reminded them that they were not yet invincible, and the surprise motivated them to win their next two games, the return against Villa and a home win over Nottingham Forest. Results came in groups. There would be a run of successes, followed by a run of failures but, over all, Leeds were in touch for the title.

Their League Cup campaign ended abruptly in the third round when they were beaten 4–2 at home by West Bromwich Albion. Revenge was sought and gained when Albion visited some weeks later for a First Division fixture, Leeds winning 4–0. That was not the only heavy defeat that the side inflicted on others. West Ham were beaten 5–0, and Nottingham Forest lost 4–0 on their own ground, and there were decisive victories over Everton, Arsenal, Blackburn and Newcastle. There was also a 6–1 demolition of Northampton at Elland Road. A home defeat by Fulham was a minor hiccup.

'We worked really hard that season,' said Billy. 'I think we had too much on our plate in the end. We had to have a replay in our Fairs Cup semi-final and I think it was just too much for us. We only took one point from our last two League matches and that meant that Liverpool were able to clean up and confirm themselves as champions. We had, once again, gone close in two competitions as we had almost reached the final of the Fairs Cup and we had also finished as runners-up in the League again. The papers were talking about us being the bridesmaids again and it was beginning to annoy us.'

The following season Leeds were in Europe once again. With England having won the World Cup, games against foreign clubs had a different aura. They were certainly tough matches but Leeds progressed – although this time it did seem to be at the expense of their League form. After the first round of their Fairs Cup campaign, they were beaten 1–0 at home by Southampton. The defence was being stretched and something had to give. On 7 November Leeds played at West Ham in the League Cup and it all went horribly wrong.

'West Ham had just put six goals past Fulham and Johnny Byrne, their outstanding scorer, was holding court with the press before their game against us. Our coach pulled in as he was talking to them and he was asked for his prediction of the result. He jokingly said, "We'll knock 'em for six like we did Fulham on Saturday." His prediction was quite wrong. West Ham did not knock us for six – they got seven!

'We couldn't believe what was happening to us. John Sissons hit a hat-trick in just over half an hour, and Geoff Hurst also got a hat-trick with Martin Peters being the other scorer. It all fell apart for us and I'm still not sure why. David Harvey was deputizing for Gary Sprake who was injured, but we could not blame him for the seven goals. We just did not perform. We went out of the League Cup again and all I had to show for the game was a booking.'

The booking was not for petulance. Billy Bremner was urging on his team-mates right to the end. His booking was for being overenthusiastic in the tackle, not for trying to gain some sort of revenge. The result was the worst since Leeds lost 8–1 to Stoke City in 1934. Less than two weeks later they went down 5–0 at Liverpool. On Boxing Day Leeds were cheered up by a 5–0 win over Newcastle at Elland Road and, in the final reckoning of the League season, they were fourth in the table – five points behind champions Manchester United. The FA Cup had been denied them at the semi-final stage, and the Inter-Cities Fairs Cup saw them reach the final, only to be beaten. Once again they had been very near to success in various competitions and yet the silverware had slipped from their grasp just when it seemed that 'Leeds United' were about to be engraved upon the trophy.

'When we started the 1967/68 season, we were hurting,' said Billy. 'We were getting really fed up with not winning anything despite getting so close. We also had a few critics to silence so we were more determined than ever to make sure that, by the end of this season, we would have something to show our supporters. We began quietly enough in our First Division campaign – we won some and we lost some. We did have a few spectacular wins that season, however, the best being a 7–0 win over Chelsea. The fans loved that one – but no more than we did ourselves. Albert Johanneson started the rout, then Jimmy Greenhoff, Jack Charlton, Peter Lorimer and Eddie Gray took it to five. Marvin Hinton scored an own goal and I added the last one. It buried the memory of our defeat at West Ham the year before. Later in the season we had two 5–0 wins in successive games against Fulham and South-ampton, so we were not short of goals. They didn't help us win the championship though.'

Leeds finished fourth again and, as before, they were five points adrift of the champions, Manchester City. They had been knocked out of the FA Cup at the semi-final stage but there was still a promise fulfilled when they worked their way through the various rounds of the League Cup until they arrived at Wembley on 2 March 1968 to play against Arsenal in the final.

'It was only the second League Cup Final to be held at Wembley and, now that it was being treated as some kind of showpiece, there was an extra incentive to make it. There were almost 100,000 in the stadium and, of course, there were the usual television cameras there. The game didn't really match up to expectations as the two defences dominated the match. It was Terry Cooper who hit the only goal of the match and, strictly speaking, he was a defender too, so that gives some idea as to what the game was like.

'What was strange about it was that Terry had told us before the game that, for the three nights leading up to the final, he had had the same dream that he would be scoring the winner at Wembley. We all laughed at that, of course, but, sure enough, with just over a quarter of an hour gone, Terry got a loose ball on the edge of the Arsenal box and thumped in a terrific shot. When the final whistle went more than an hour later we all knew that his dream had come true and we were pretty impressed, I can tell you.

'At long last we had won something, and I was as proud as anything when we paraded the League Cup back in Leeds. At the Town Hall there were tens of thousands of Leeds fans massed around the building having a gigantic party. Our season was not yet over but we enjoyed every moment of that celebration. We then reached the final of the Fairs Cup for the second successive season. Rather unusually, the final of this competition was always played over two legs at the start of the following season. I did not enjoy that very much. I liked everything wrapped up at the end of a season, not spilling over into the next one.'

Bremner was by now a full Scottish international and life was very full. He never lost an ounce of his enthusiasm though, and during the close season he spent much of his time looking forward to getting on with the next challenge.

'He could be a dreadful fidget at times,' said Vicky, his wife. 'He was always great with the family and he loved to go back to Scotland to see his relatives and pals up there, but he never liked to go very long without kicking a football. If he saw some kids playing he would be just as likely to join in with them. That was Billy – he loved his family, but football was his life.'

Early in the 1968/69 season, Leeds won the Inter-Cities Fairs Cup. Within a week they were commencing an unsuccessful bid to retain the trophy. There were other fish to fry as well, however. The club made early exits from both the FA Cup and the League Cup. Their eyes were firmly fixed on the League championship.

'We were all aware that Leeds had never won the League championship,' said Billy. 'The ambition to change that was overwhelming. We were feared the length and breadth of the country and we felt that we just had to be champions soon. The title race that season was an exciting one – and not just for Leeds United. Liverpool, Everton, Arsenal and ourselves were all involved and seemed to take it in turns to take the top spot. It was like a leading pack in a horse race continually jostling each other while the rest of the field remained strung out behind them. In the first half of the season we had two defeats we would rather forget. A 3–1 loss at Manchester City and a 5–1 at Burnley. As it turned out, however, they were to be our only League losses of the season – and we beat Burnley 6–1 at Elland Road, so that paid them back. We also beat City in the return by 1–0.

'There were one or two games in which we didn't play very well, but we still managed to take the lead and we kept our noses in front, even during the bad times. When it came to the week before Easter we were still just about hanging on to our lead. Easter was always crunch time. Liverpool were hot on our heels, although Everton and Arsenal had drifted a bit. When Liverpool won away to Queen's Park Rangers while we were drawing 0–0 at Wolves, they breathed even harder down our necks. They drew their next game and so did we. The following weekend Johnny Giles scored the only goal of our game, but Roger Hunt did the same thing for Liverpool. The tension was mounting all the time. Although we had a five-point advantage, Liverpool had a game in hand and probably an easier list of remaining fixtures, apart from one – they had to play us at Anfield.

'Going to Anfield was our penultimate game of the season.

We needed at least a draw to confirm that we were champions. Liverpool knew that, if they beat us, they were still in with a reasonable chance. There were 53,750 people inside Anfield for that Monday night game – and at least 2,000 others locked outside. The game was one of the most thrilling that I have ever played in. We were really wound up in the right way before the game. We knew what we had to do and, mostly, that meant keeping our cool and playing our normal professional game.

'The game was played at a lightning pace with Liverpool doing their best to break down our defence. However, Jack Charlton and Norman Hunter were tremendous and held it all together. In fact Gary Sprake, in goal, was almost having an easy night because nothing got through the defence. We nearly sneaked one at the other end when I had a shot deflected. The minutes ticked away and when the final whistle blew I enjoyed one of the greatest experiences of my football life.

'Up to that moment the Liverpool fans had been solidly behind their team, roaring them on to a possible victory. Once that final whistle went and they knew that the game and the title race was over, they put away their bias and gave us a standing ovation. We even went on a lap of honour and they cheered us as if we were their own team. It was a fantastic moment and one of the greatest gestures that I have ever experienced. The Liverpool players were also sporting and generous in their congratulations and even Bill Shankly came down to our dressing room and said: "You're worthy champions – a great side. Well done boys." He then shook Don Revie's hand warmly.

'The boss came over and ruffled my hair as I sat at my place. I was laughing along with everyone else, but I was also having my own thoughts about the long, hard slog that had, at last, brought us to this moment. It wasn't about one game, or one season, it had been five years of frustration, sweat, toil, criticism and desire. We had finally made it and done so in style.'

They had too. When they finished the season with a 1–0 win over Nottingham Forest at Elland Road, it meant that Leeds United had won the championship with a record number of points and had been undefeated at home all season.

'We had answered the critics in the best way possible. It had been said that we had kicked our way out of the Second Division, to have kicked most of our First Division opponents, and generally to have been undesirables in the game. We had often been hurt by that criticism because we knew that we were better than that. That wonderful night at Anfield saw our burning faith in ourselves justified. At last we were well and truly vindicated.'

That, of course, is not the end of the championship story. It was the first of two occasions when Billy Bremner would be handed the trophy.

Allan Clarke joined the club in June 1969, Leeds paying a British record £165,000 to sign him from Leicester. He and Billy became firm friends instantly and, of course, Clarke brought extra firepower to the side, making Leeds even more awesome.

'I wondered a little bit what Allan would be like as a team-mate,' recalled Billy. 'I had played against him and knew what his ability was like, but he also had a reputation for being the sort of person who kept himself to himself and didn't have much to do with the rest of the squad. But I had no need to worry about his contribution to team spirit. It was soon quite obvious that he wanted to be a real team-mate. He was quickly nicknamed "Sniffer" because of his great talent of being able to sniff out a half-chance and put the ball into the back of the net.

'We were all amazed by him. Mick Jones, who had been with the club for a little while, was also a fantastic player and scorer – but everyone knew that Mick was around. Allan's game was totally different. He was so crafty that he would just seem to disappear, then, from nowhere, the ball was in the net – and who had scored? Allan Clarke.

'Apart from the fact that he was a great professional, a

superb player, and a really nice guy, there was something else I had in common with Allan Clarke. I envied him because he had been at Fulham some years earlier and had played alongside Johnny Haynes who had been another one of my heroes – my favourite English player in fact. I would love to have played in the same team as him, and Allan had. So I used to get him to talk about the great man and try to get an insider's view of him. I wasn't disappointed. It was as a result of those chats, I think, that Allan and I became such good pals, and our families have been close ever since.'

Allan Clarke, for his part, felt the same about Billy Bremner.

'He became like a brother to me. When I first joined Leeds I was delighted by the family atmosphere of the club. I was worried that they all thought that I was a bit of a loner, but I wasn't. Billy and the rest made me feel very welcome right from my first day and we spent a lot of time together, socially as well as in our work. Billy on the pitch was a human dynamo. I don't think that there has ever been a player who earned respect and admiration more than Billy Bremner. There are other legends, but Billy achieved his status in the game against all the odds. He was like a fan when we talked about Johnny Haynes, and he told me that if he made a bad pass he used to mutter to himself, "Johnny Haynes wouldn't have wasted that ball." Away from the pitch, he was a lovely guy who would do anything for you. I was deeply shocked when he died, Billy and I were room-mates for years and remained close friends ever since we first met. I still sometimes have to remind myself that he is no longer with us. I used to enjoy his company so much and, when our two families were together, it was great.'

Clarke's arrival heralded another new era for Leeds. He immediately became a great partner to fellow striker Mick Jones, and they developed an incredible understanding. Add to that the partnership between Bremner and Giles, and a defence in which Jack Charlton was a rock, and it is no wonder that Leeds were so formidable.

The 1969/70 season was once again exciting but fruitless. The club reached the FA Cup Final but lost to Chelsea, who had earlier knocked them out of the League Cup. They reached the semi-finals of the European Cup before bowing out to Celtic and, in the race for the League championship, they again recorded some tremendous results with Lorimer, Clarke, Jones and Giles scoring fifty-nine goals between them. Nottingham Forest were beaten 4–1 and 6–1, Chelsea and West Bromwich were both hit for five, and Ipswich and West Ham were four-goal victims. But perhaps the most significant result was a 3–2 defeat at Everton in their seventh game of the season. It ended a run of thirty-four League matches, home and away, without defeat. In the final reckoning, it also helped Everton on their way to the League championship – Leeds finishing second.

The 1970/71 season had a breakthrough of a different sort for Leeds as they found success in Europe for the first time. But on the domestic front there was little or no progress in the cup competitions and, once again, Leeds finished as runners-up in the League.

'It was disappointing not to take the championship again,' said Billy. 'We were just one point behind Arsenal. Near the end of the season we lost at home to West Bromwich, a game we should definitely have won. Had we done so we would have been champions again. Our goal difference was the same as Arsenal's and it was even more frustrating than usual. Not that I would want to take anything away from Arsenal. They were a very fine side and they did the Double that year, which was a wonderful achievement for them. We could not complain about our season because we had done well and, in the years since we had returned to the First Division, we had twice finished fourth, been runners-up three times and had also won the title, so I think we had proved our point. We took consolation from our success in Europe, but I have always maintained that it is possible for a club to win the League championship, the FA Cup, the League Cup and a European trophy, all in the same season. It has never been done yet by an English club but I am convinced that it will one day.'

Bremner had Leeds in mind when he said that, of course. It was a typical statement that demonstrated his determination and will to win. He honestly believed that it was possible and who could argue with him?

Crowd problems meant that Leeds were forced to play four of their home matches on neutral grounds in the 1971/72 season. Nevertheless, they were unbeaten in those games and, when they returned to Elland Road, their only home defeat all season was in the League Cup when they were beaten 1–0 by West Ham after extra-time. Their form was nothing short of brilliant and, when you consider that they put seven past Southampton, six past Nottingham Forest and five past both Newcastle and Manchester United, it makes you wonder why they once again finished as runners-up and not as champions.

'We were pushed out by fixture planning, I am convinced of that,' said Bremner. 'We played in the FA Cup Final against Arsenal at Wembley on the Saturday and then, two nights later, we had to finish our League fixtures with an away match against Wolves. We won the Cup and we needed just one point from the Wolves game to clinch the championship – which would have meant that we won the Double. Liverpool were also in the hunt but they were behind us by a point and had an inferior goal average. Derby were actually top but they did not expect to win the championship. In fact, their players had already gone on holiday by this time.

'While we were at Wolves, Liverpool were at Arsenal. We were quite drained after winning the FA Cup and we just could not get it together at Wolves. We lost 2–1. Liverpool had a 0–0 draw with Arsenal, so they finished up on the same number of points as us – and that meant that Derby were champions after all. We were annoyed about it. Taking nothing away from Derby who had played well, we thought that it was a little unjust not to give us at least a few days to recover from Wembley. I'm sure that's what cost us the Double.'

In the 1972/73 season, Leeds competed in the European Cup Winners' Cup and, once again, Billy Bremner led them to within a whisker of success. However, they ended up as beaten finalists, as they did in the FA Cup. Liverpool had knocked them out of the League Cup and, despite hammering Arsenal 6–1 at home on the last day of the season, Leeds had to be content with third place in the League – their lowest final placing for five years.

The following season was to be the last under the direction of Don Revie. In the summer of 1973 there had been strong suggestions that he was to quit and become manager of Everton, but once again he turned down the chance and remained at Elland Road.

'I was relieved about that,' said Bremner. 'We had come a long way together and we had consistently been so close to winning the championship again that we felt that it could only be a matter of time. We didn't want any major changes to spoil things. I was very confident that we could do it, but I also knew that it was vital that Don Revie remained in charge. As it was he did stay and we got off to a flyer in the League. I think we won our first seven games and went right through to late February before we lost a League match. We set the pace for everyone else to follow. We opened a big gap between ourselves and the rest and, even when we had a brief spell of three defeats in a row in March, we still kept our lead.

'We had won the championship before the season was over. On the night when we actually won the title, we were not even playing. Liverpool were at home to Arsenal and lost 1–0, which left us in an unbeatable position. It was a great feeling, but the real party came three days later in Shepherds Bush, London. It was our last game of the season and we were away to Queen's Park Rangers. Loftus Road saw its biggest crowd of the season because half of Leeds had invaded the capital and, for us, it was like a home game. Allan Clarke scored the only goal of the game so we finished on a high.

'When the game was over we were all hugging each other

and the boss joined in. It was a great moment, but a sad one too because the break-up was about to take place.'

Whatever the future held, Billy Bremner was captain of the champions, the best team in the country – and arguably the best Leeds team of all time.

7

BILLY AND DON

After the dust had settled following the parties to celebrate
Leeds United's second championship Don Revie was on his
way to take up a new challenge as manager of England. Most
great and successful teams have thrived on the rapport
between manager and captain. The great Leeds side of the late
1960s and early 1970s had just such a partnership – between
manager Don Revie and skipper Billy Bremner.

They became team-mates at Elland Road when Bremner was
playing his first few games for the club. Their friendship blos-
somed and survived even when Bremner's impatience and
homesickness got the better of him and he made several transfer requests after Revie had become manager.

Bremner never lost sight of the part that Revie played in his
career. The hardest part for Don Revie was the transition that
he had to make from being a player and 'one of the lads' to
becoming 'the boss'.

'We all wondered if the appointment would upset things,'
remembered Billy. 'Whether he would begin to wield the big
stick in his new position or whether it would make for a better
team spirit. Don himself took it all in his stride.'

Billy hardly helped in that period of Revie's transition from
player to boss. It was at this time that Bremner was at his most
unsettled. He continually harangued the new boss for a transfer and to be allowed to return to Scotland.

'He must have been sick of the sight and sound of me. Every
time I bumped into him and I opened my mouth, he knew

Starting out in 1960 – just look at those boots. (COLORSPORT)

Billy the acrobat wows Chelsea. (COLORSPORT)

The 1970 Leeds United team (above). (POPPERFOTO)

Billy gets ready to make a defence-splitting pass against Queen's Park Rangers in 1974 (right). (COLORSPORT)

Another triumph. This time Manchester United were the victims in a 1969 game (below). (COLORSPORT)

After drawing in the 1970 FA Cup final at Wembley both Bremner and Revie know they must do it all again. (COLORSPORT)

Revie prepares his men for extra time in the 1970 FA Cup final replay. (COLORSPORT)

Billy believes the ref has gone deaf in a 1971 game against Coventry (above). (COLORSPORT)

Who me? Billy denies everything after the 1970 FA Cup final (right). (COLORSPORT)

A lighter moment in 1971 against West Bromwich Albion (below). (COLORSPORT)

By Royal Appointment! Prince Philip meets the lads before the 1972 FA Cup final. (POPPERFOTO)

It's ours! Billy parades the FA Cup after beating Arsenal in the 1972 final. (COLORSPORT)

The 1974 Charity Shield, during which Bremner and Keegan were famously sent off. (COLORSPORT)

Bremner scores the vital goal which takes Leeds to the Championship in 1974. (COLORSPORT)

Skill and determination – the Bremner formula for success.
(COLORSPORT)

The Championship is won and Billy leads the celebrations.
(COLORSPORT)

It's in the net and
Bremner's scored again!
(COLORSPORT)

Jack Charlton and Billy
Bremner. How could
Leeds ever lose?
(POPPERFOTO)

what was coming. "Let me go . . . let me go . . . let me go . . ." I must have sounded like a long-playing record.'

Don Revie's solution to the problems he had with his young player is a prime example of the sympathy and understanding that Revie possessed, and it led to the time when Billy Bremner and Vicky got married and set up their home in Leeds. Bremner's relationship with Revie continued to improve over the years.

'The relationship between player and manager is very important and at Leeds we had it right because there was such a family spirit. When I was a young lad I sometimes used to babysit for Don and his wife Elsie, and you always knew that, if you had a problem, you only had to pick up the phone and either the boss or one of your team-mates would be there.

'I remember when I was courting Vicky, I was returning from Scotland when I had a crash just north of Scotch Corner at four in the morning. I telephoned the boss and he said, "Hang on there, I'm coming up right away!" He just got out of bed and even though it was that time in the morning he drove straight up to collect me.

'He was never a tough disciplinarian despite his outward image. If you stepped out of line you knew you were for the chopping block, but he never had to rant and rave. He commanded respect because he gave respect and treated his players as men. Though we were allowed to dress in casual clothes for travelling away, we always had to remember that we were representing the club and had to be presentable. We were not allowed to have very long hair. We didn't have to look like convicts but we were expected to look neat.

'He was always very superstitious and would often wear the same suit game after game while we were winning. His favourite was a blue one. I was a bit superstitious for a while, like most players. I used to do things like borrow Norman Hunter's comb, putting my pants on last and things like that. I was cured when we were narrowly pipped for three major trophies in one season. I realized then that it was not worth all the trouble – what will be will be.

71

'Superstition or not, Don Revie was nobody's fool. He made Leeds United great again and after he had left things began to decline. When he went to the England job he did not have a great success as he had done at Elland Road – mostly I think because he did not have the daily contact with players and therefore could not develop that family spirit which worked so well at Leeds. For my money, Don Revie was one of the greatest managers of all time and he certainly played a key part in my career. When he was awarded the OBE in January 1971, nobody was more pleased than me. It was an honour he thoroughly deserved.'

When he was alive, Don Revie was often asked about Billy Bremner and he never failed to heap praises on the young Scottish prince who became a king. He once remarked on his luck.

'Billy Bremner has won some very important tosses for Leeds United. His luck at the spin of a disc, which used to decide cup ties in European football that ended level on aggregate scores, helped us to go through against both Bologna and Naples in the Fairs Cup.

'But there's a lot more to being a good captain than being lucky at the toss, and Billy Bremner had all the necessary qualities. Billy's approach to the game was terrific. Confidence flowed out of him, inspiring the players around him – he made everybody play – he was all heart, courage and power. He hated to get beat, he never pulled out of a tackle and his skill on the ball was second to none.

'Billy was the only player in my experience who could switch play when running flat out by hitting a diagonal pass with a cross-behind leg action. Perhaps you have to be playing to appreciate him fully.'

Revie did not just think that Billy was a good captain, he reckoned him to be one of the greatest in the history of football. The Football Writers' Association obviously took his leadership qualities into account too when they voted him 'Footballer of the Year'.

Revie's own thoughts even looked beyond Bremner's career

as captain of Leeds United.

'I believe that the extra demands that are being made on club captains will eventually help them to become equally famous and capable managers. There are exceptions of course but, even in the old days when a captain's responsibilities were more limited in scope, the good skipper invariably developed into a good manager.

'Nowadays, with many more duties thrown into a captain's curriculum, such a role must be an even better apprenticeship for management.'

Revie also recognized the need for communication between captain and manager and vice versa. He saw it as a vital aspect of any club's hope for success. Communication made for harmony and understanding in the dressing room, which in turn could lead on to the success for which every club strives.

'The sort of understanding that existed between Billy Bremner and myself played no small part in achieving the family atmosphere at Elland Road. We had respect for each other and we trusted each other all along the line. That trust and respect existed in no small measure between Billy and his team-mates, reflected in his leadership and his playing abilities.'

A manager organizes the tactical approach to any game but without someone in authority to interpret his tactical thoughts for the rest of the team, and to carrying out of those thoughts while the game is in progress, there would be no proper team organization.

'Never in the history of the game,' said Revie, 'has so much preparation gone into matches before they even start. Yet even the best laid plans often require some reappraisal out on the park – and that is where a captain like Billy Bremner proved his value. One of his major jobs was to be able to read the situation out there and to adjust the tactics to the situation. Our pre-match discussion had laid down guidelines for the game but we had to expect our opponents to formulate plans of their own to stop ours from working smoothly. If our team ran into trouble, Billy had the responsibility of changing or adapting the tactics.

Because he had such respect from his team-mates, he was able to draw on the advice of some of the senior players such as Johnny Giles, Norman Hunter and Jack Charlton to help him out – but the ultimate responsibility was his alone.'

That responsibility is a far cry from the days when the captain's job was ended after he had called 'heads' or 'tails' at the start of a game. Nowadays, and in Billy Bremner's day too, there is a lot more to a captain's job, off the field as well as on it. Don Revie had more than a little to say on this subject.

'At Elland Road we always prided ourselves on the fact that young players soon settled down happily. Every player, however long or short a time he had been there, was aware that he could come and knock on my door at any time.

'Sometimes, however, a young player who had just joined the club could be a little afraid of knocking on my door – or on the doors of any of the managerial staff. It is then that the captain proves his worth. He has to be able to discern a worried look and then be able to discover the reason for it, so that he can put the player in touch with the best person to help.

'On one occasion, Billy discovered that one of the young Leeds players had not told anybody that his father had just died. We soon had the lad back home and Billy himself saw to it that a wreath was sent on behalf of the first team. Billy was the club captain and he never forgot anybody. Every Christmas he used to have a whip round among the players to buy every-body on the staff a present – nightwatchmen, tea-makers, laundry workers . . . the lot.

'On the occasion of our visit to Wembley when we were playing Chelsea in the FA Cup Final, he made sure that the players did not forget the backroom boys. There were gifts for the coaching staff and the club doctor.'

Being a captain is so much more than being a good foot-baller. Of course, being a good footballer is a necessary qualification but then again, so is a whole host of other abilities and qualities. What was it about Billy Bremner that made him such a good captain?

'Billy was such a good skipper because he not only had this

tremendous leadership quality, dedication and drive, but also an amazing ability which every player he came into contact with respected. By his own example he always brought out the correct response from his colleagues and that is something which is so important in a captain.

'That response can make an enormous difference to a team's performance. One player may not be doing what is needed of him and the captain has to know why he is going wrong and, what is more important, how to put him on the right track. In order to do that he has to be fully conversant with the make-up of all his team-mates. He has to know immediately how best to approach the problem in a way that will provide the best solution for the player and for the rest of the team.

'Some players respond best to a good old-fashioned "ticking-off", while others will become upset and flustered by such treatment. These need to be encouraged rather than browbeaten. There was nobody better than Billy Bremner when he was at Leeds at diagnosing the best course of treatment to administer.'

Don Revie knew Billy Bremner for a good many years. From the start, when Billy was still a teenager, Revie could see his great potential. They played alongside each other and Revie encouraged him. Later, when Revie became manager, he continued to encourage him through the awkward first years of his time at Leeds. He watched as Billy grew in experience and stature, fulfilling all that potential that he had spotted in those early days.

'Billy and I first got together in January 1960. He was just seventeen when we formed a right-wing partnership for Leeds at Chelsea in a First Division game. Billy was out on the wing and I was inside-forward. We shared a hotel room for that trip and before the match we talked a lot about the dedication that you have to put into the game.

'I could see from the start that Billy had the ability to go right to the top. I wanted to see if he would use that ability. I didn't need to worry. He had no trouble with the big-time atmosphere, he was confident – even cheeky – in that first debut game. As early as that I predicted that he would be playing for Scotland before he was twenty. To be truthful, he didn't become a full international quite as early as that – although I am convinced that he would have done so had he been playing for a Scottish club and not for an English one – especially one that did not belong to the fashionable set of those days.

'Billy has to go down in history as one of the greatest players of all time and his being captain of Leeds United has helped him to add to his great ability. Good captains have so much more to do than the rest of the players. They have to set an example in training and fitness. They must play a big part in public relations through interviews on radio and television. When a captain does that he is setting the whole image of his club.

'Billy has put his club before himself on innumerable occasions. One thing that many used to say about him was that he would play even if he had a broken leg, and it was certainly true that he played with many injuries which would have kept many a lesser player out of action. His reasons for doing this were never for self-praise, but because he recognized the effect that his absence would have on the rest of the team in a vital match – especially so when one or more of the other key players had already been ruled out. This happened so often because of the heavy casualty rate that Leeds endured as a result of being so successful and therefore having to play so many extra games.

'Billy Bremner, in my view, was more entitled than any of his contemporaries to be called the "Captain Courageous". He turned games to Leeds' favour so many times by going into the thick of the battle when nobody would have blamed him for taking a less prominent part in the action.

'In one particular clash with Everton he damaged a knee, but he still hobbled into the Everton penalty area when a corner kick was being taken and, from only half a chance, he hit a fantastic winner. Once again his courage and know-how had proved to be invaluable. Captains and players like him had a value beyond price.'

When Billy Bremner received that 'Footballer of the Year' award in 1970 he was almost lost for words. He recognized the fact that he had been considered for the honour because of the way he had harnessed his aggression and passion and had transformed himself into a world-class footballer – but he also paid tribute to the people who had played a major role in helping him to do it.

'It is a truly great honour to receive this,' he said. 'Especially when I look at the list of the names of the players who have gone before me. To me, though, this award has not just got Billy Bremner's name on it. It has the names of all the Leeds United players and, most especially, our boss Don Revie who has made it all possible.'

Revie led the applause and Bremner applauded him in return. The partnership had mutual admiration and respect. Above all else – it worked to perfection.

8

EUROPE

There is no doubt that in the early 1960s Leeds United was a club that was looked upon by the vast majority as also-rans. Apart from a youth tournament in Holland, Leeds had never won anything outstanding – unless, of course, you count promotion from the Second Division as something special. The problem seemed to be that they had always yo-yoed back and forth and that seemed to be the set formula for the club. But what about that youth tournament? Billy Bremner was there.

'I was a member of the team which did win the first trophy which ever decorated the Elland Road sideboard. Bill Lambton was the manager of Leeds United in those days and he had already instituted the youth policy which was to flower so successfully under Don Revie. Well, we went to Holland to compete in that youth tournament. Really, we all felt as if we were going along for the ride and for some good experience. There was myself, Gary Sprake, Paul Reaney, Norman Hunter and others in the crop of youngsters who went on to make the grade in the First Division.

'We found ourselves in the final after several preliminary games and had to take on Birmingham – strange opponents considering that we had travelled to Holland to meet them. At the end of the ninety minutes we had beaten them. Harry Reynolds came into the dressing room after that game and shed tears of joy. It was, he said, his finest moment as chairman of the club. There was the chairman, visibly moved by the fact that a bunch of kids had managed to achieve some-thing in the name of Leeds United. And there we were, tickled pink, and somebody mentioned that it had all been great and weren't those fish and chips smashing last night!

'"What fish and chips?" Harry Reynolds wanted to know. So we explained that the previous evening we had wandered along to a little café and found that they were serving fish and chips, so we went in and had a feast. "Then that's what we'll do right now," he said, and he was as good as his word. He took us back to the little café and there the players, and the chairman of Leeds United, celebrated the first time that the club had ever won anything with an after-match banquet of fish and chips!'

When Leeds sprang out of the Second Division at the end of the 1964 season, they did manage to sweep upwards near to the top of the First Division, but even then that first season ended with them being runners-up in the League to Manchester United on goal average.

It wasn't until 1968, when Leeds played Arsenal in the League Cup Final at Wembley, that they finally achieved a measure of success. Many people said that it was the drabbest-ever Wembley final but, to Leeds, it was a spring-board to further honours.

Having finished as runners-up in the First Division at the end of the 1964/65 season, Leeds were able to make their debut in Europe, in the Inter-Cities Fairs Cup.

'I had the honour of scoring our first goal in Europe,' said Bremner. 'We were drawn against Torino in the first round of the competition, and the first leg was at Elland Road. It was a tough game, as we expected, but we won 2–1. I scored our first and Alan Peacock hit our second. Although it was a very physical game, we were not prepared for what was to follow in the return leg a week later. The Italian side seemed deter-mined to win at any cost. They failed because the 0–0 final score meant that we went through with the 2–1 aggregate in our favour – but there was an incident during the game which had me in tears of distress and sheer anger. It was the time I saw the greatest little player in my days at Leeds United chopped down ruthlessly. The player was fellow Scot wee Bobby Collins and the foul broke his thigh bone.

'I was so upset that I found myself weeping and, had the chance come my way, I would have "done" the player who had so crippled my team-mate. Thousands of words have been written about Bobby Collins, and the grand work that he did in putting Leeds United on the map, but those words never said the half of it.

'The foul was quite the worst that I had ever seen and when I realized what had happened, I must admit that I lost my head completely and snarled at the player who had done it, "I'll kill you for this." Believe me, I really meant it at the time, too. That player probably didn't understand what I had said, but he certainly got the message and stayed well away from me for the rest of the match. Perhaps it was as well – for me as much as for him!

'That was all such a long time ago, but it really taught me something. I have never since that day gone onto the field with such feelings as I had then. That day, blinding anger and passion got the better of me and obscured my better judgement. If I had tangled with that Italian player in a fight for possession of the ball, I could not have been responsible for my actions. The foul had been so unnecessary and was so obviously vindictive – Bobby had been ten yards from the ball when he had been, quite literally, jumped on.

'I think that must have been the only time that anyone has broken his femur on the football field. It is the biggest bone in the body and takes a tremendous impact, such as a car crash, to cause such an injury. When they carried Bobby Collins off to hospital that day, I was convinced that it was the last time we would ever see him on a football pitch. If anyone had said to me that he would be back, and not only walking but playing for the first team at Leeds United again, I would have snarled in his face: "Who do you think you're kidding?"

'But Bobby being Bobby, he did come back and he played in

the very last game of that season. What a fighter, and what a player.'

Bremner scored in the next round against SC Leipzig, which was a repeat of the first round as far as the result was concerned. Leeds won the first leg 2–1 away and then drew 0–0 at Elland Road, enough to move on to a third-round tie against Valencia. Once again there was a 2–1 aggregate. Ujpesti Dozsa were the next victims. A 4–1 lead from the home leg and a 1–1 away draw took Leeds into a semi-final against Real Zaragoza. After the two legs, the scoreline read 2–2 and so a replay was necessary. The Spanish side won 3–1 and that was the end of the first Leeds sortie into Europe.

'Naturally we were disappointed, but we took heart from the fact that it was our first attempt, and we had learned a great deal. We didn't feel that we had disgraced ourselves and we were determined to do even better next time. We were totally confident that there would be a next time.'

There was indeed a next time – the very next season, in fact. Once again Billy Bremner opened the scoring. Leeds had been given a bye to the second round in which they were drawn to play DWS Amsterdam. The first leg was away and, after Bremner scored the first goal, Leeds won 3–1. Back at Elland Road, a hat-trick by Albert Johanneson led the way to a 5–1 victory in the second leg and a comfortable passage to the third round, where Leeds faced Valencia for the second successive season. This time Leeds won with a 3–1 aggregate score.

The fourth round was against Bologna and, after each club had won 1–0, the tie had to be settled with the toss of a coin. Leeds made it and faced Kilmarnock in the semi-final. Rod Belfitt was the hat-trick hero this time as Leeds won 4–2 at home. The 0–0 away result was good enough to put Leeds in the final against Dinamo Zagreb.

'We took the game to them in the first leg, but we could not break down their defence. They had a couple of breaks and scored each time. We were not too upset by the 2–0 score because we thought we could overcome that in the second leg at Elland Road. Once again their defence held and the score was 0–0 – which meant that we finished as runners-up. I was upset by that but we had done our best.'

Leeds made it again to the Fairs Cup competition in the following year and this time opened with a first-round tie against Spora Luxembourg.

'The first leg of the tie was away,' recalled Bremner. 'We'd never heard of Spora and we really thumped them. I suppose they wished that they had never heard of us after we finished pumping goals into their net. Hot-shot Peter Lorimer slammed the ball home four times, once from the penalty spot. Jimmy Greenhoff scored a couple and Paul Madeley, Mick Jones and myself hit one apiece. The final score was 9–0.

'The return leg was almost an anti-climax. It was at Elland Road a fortnight later and we could only manage to score seven. This time Albert Johanneson was the hat-trick man, while Jimmy Greenhoff got another couple. Peter Lorimer and Terry Cooper had to be satisfied with a goal each.'

With Spora being a team of amateurs, just about rating as Central League material in this country, it is not surprising that Leeds United won, and yet despite that huge goal aggregate, Leeds still came in for a fair bit of criticism.

'We were criticized because we didn't beat the record that had been set up by Cologne two years earlier. Like us, they just ran riot. They beat a team from Luxembourg called Union Sportiv. It was pointed out that we missed at least three sitters, and that we could, and should, have eclipsed that Cologne record. Still, we equalled it, so I don't see why anyone should have grumbled.'

The next round brought Leeds face to face with a team that was more than capable of holding its own. At the end of November 1967, they flew out to Yugoslavia to meet Partizan Belgrade. Partizan had beaten Manchester United in the semi-final of the European Cup in April 1966, when United were favourites to win.

'According to everyone it should have been United's turn to win the European Cup, yet Partizan took everything that they could throw at them and still managed to win through to the final on a 2–1 aggregate.

'I heard that when Manchester United went out there, Partizan played as if they were up against world beaters for the first forty-five minutes. After that it was as if someone had told them that Matt Busby's men were mere mortals after all. Manchester United should have been ahead by a couple of goals at half-time, by all accounts, instead they went home trailing by two second-half goals.

'We, at Leeds United, were not prepared to settle for such a sucker punch, and had no intention of suffering the same fate as Manchester United. Every Leeds player was under orders to work and run, and put 100 per cent into everything. We obeyed to the letter. We chased and we harried and we never gave Partizan the time to breathe. Partizan were a good team all right, and they were ready to give as much as they took, but they couldn't match us for pace, punch and staying power. They hit one goal, but Peter Lorimer and Rod Belfitt hit one each to give us a winning scoreline of 2–1.

'In the return game we intended to thrash the living daylights out of them and we set about doing it in the first half. We mounted attack after attack on their goal. However, it wasn't possible to keep up the pace we had set ourselves and, by the second half, we just had to take it a little bit easier. Peter Lorimer scored again, but so did they and the game ended in a 1–1 draw. That took us through to round three on a 3–2 aggregate.'

The draw saw Leeds United up against the club to which Billy Bremner had once hoped to be transferred – Hibernian. Hibs had beaten Napoli by five goals in the previous round at Easter Road and most Scots were laying odds that the same thing was about to happen to Leeds. Five days before Christmas the first leg was played at Elland Road.

'We gave what must have been the worst performance ever in a European competition. Gary Sprake, in goal, was almost a spectator but the rest of us couldn't do much right when it came to getting the ball into Hibernian's net. In the end, it took a Scot, in the shape of Eddie Gray, finally to score the only goal of the match.

'The second week in January we went up to Easter Road, far from happy with our slender lead, yet we were determined that the same thing was not going to happen to us that had happened to Napoli. We found the pitch to be rock-hard, which did not augur well for good football. We didn't play much better than on our previous encounter, but we did put up a tremendous show of sheer endeavour. We risked injury, we fought for every ball. Hibs did manage to score, but Jack Charlton got one for us and so, once again, we were through to the next round on aggregate, by the odd goal.'

The win against Hibernian took Leeds United through to the quarter-finals, where another Scottish team was waiting to face them. Glasgow Rangers were an experienced team in European competition and the first leg of the quarter-final was to be played at Ibrox. The match was relayed live by closed-circuit television to the supporters at Elland Road. It was a wet and windy day as the game started, with 80,000 chanting fans in Ibrox Stadium, ready for what they knew would be a real battle.

'We were playing our fifty-second game of the season when we faced Rangers, but we played as if it was our first. Rangers just could not get through our defence and we were well satisfied to leave Ibrox knowing that there was nothing in it, with the home game still to come.

'The return at Elland Road followed the same pattern as the first game. This time the situation was reversed, in that the closed-circuit television cameras took the game to thousands of Rangers supporters who went along to Ibrox to watch. At Elland Road we had one of our few 50,000 crowds, and they certainly got their money's worth. Just like at Ibrox, Rangers threw everything at us in the opening spell, hoping to shake us up by scoring an early goal. However, our defence held them and gradually we began to take a grip on the game. Rangers might have been a little aggrieved when their efforts did not produce even a single goal, but it wouldn't have made any difference anyway. Peter Lorimer hit one and Johnny Giles scored from the penalty spot, putting the issue beyond all doubt.'

Leeds United were now through to the semi-finals and yet again they had a Scottish team waiting to meet them. This time it was Dundee. The match was played on May Day at Dundee and ended in a 1–1 draw. It was one of the few games missed by Gary Sprake during his career at Leeds. His place was taken by David Harvey who proved to be an extremely capable deputy. The return match at Elland Road was the sixty-sixth competitive football game of the season for Leeds United.

'That return leg with Dundee wasn't much to write home about. Fewer than 24,000 spectators turned up to watch the game and we definitely looked a bit jaded. We probably were jaded after all those games. We certainly lacked lustre and didn't play anywhere near as well as we had done in our previous competition matches. However, we still managed to get the goal that mattered, through Eddie Gray, and that ensured that we were through to the final – against the Hungarian side, Ferencvaros.'

In August 1967, Don Revie had said that his ambition was for Leeds to win any two trophies – it didn't really matter which ones. Leeds were, in fact, going for four at the time – the First Division championship, the Inter-Cities Fairs Cup, the FA Cup and the League Cup. They lost their FA Cup chance at the semi-final stage in a 1–0 defeat by Chelsea, and they finished fourth in the First Division. They had won the League Cup by beating Arsenal at Wembley, which left only the Inter-Cities Fairs Cup for Don Revie to realize his ambition. The first leg was held at Elland Road and ended in a win for Leeds, with the only goal of the match scored by Mick Jones. The second leg was to be held in Budapest on the night of 11 September 1968.

'The Fairs Cup Final second leg in the giant Nep Stadium of Budapest wasn't a great game as finals go, but it was a tense one from the opening whistle to the end. 80,000

Hungarian supporters watched as Ferencvaros mounted attack after attack, and Leeds pulled out all the defensive stops. Players like Terry Cooper, Norman Hunter and Paul Madeley played like two men, Gary Sprake never made a slip in goal, and Jack Charlton used his head to superb effect in nodding away the ball which Ferencvaros persisted in thumping down the field.

'Albert and Varga of Ferencvaros certainly did their best to prise open the Leeds defence, but they couldn't manage it on their own. The Hungarian attack, too, didn't really click as a unit. A lot of the scoring attempts came from individual attempts to break through, or from chasing a long ball booted down the middle.

'Right from the kick-off, Ferencvaros left us in no doubt that they intended to bank on all-out attack. In turn, we left them in no doubt at all that they were up against a bunch of unyielding Yorkshiremen. We packed our defence so solidly that it was a full twenty minutes before any real threat approached our goal. Rakosi got through to our penalty area, which was packed with white shirts, and let loose a flyer. He was wasting his time – Terry Cooper made it all look so easy when he cleared the ball with a seemingly casual overhead kick. I have to say that I breathed a little more easily when I saw that Terry's move had been successful, I can tell you!

'A few minutes later it was Terry to the rescue again. He deflected a low, hard shot from Albert and eased the pressure once again. In fact, about thirty minutes into the game, we almost shook them with a goal out of the blue. We were awarded a free kick which was taken by Mike O'Grady. The ball went high to Mick Jones who got to it with his head. Ferencvaros had the biggest let-off of the night when the ball cannoned against the bar. After that we did try a couple of snap shots, but both were parried by the Ferencvaros keeper, Geczi, and after that we went back to our defensive tactics until the whistle blew for half-time.

'From the start of the second half we were thrown back into defence again as right winger Szoke tore down the line and whipped in an angled shot. We breathed again as Gary Sprake pulled off a tremendous save. After that we were almost caught out again when one of the Ferencvaros forwards slipped into our penalty area, kept on running, but made a smart back-pass for a team-mate to collect. For a few dangerous seconds we were all over the place and a shot went in – fortunately wide, and we could breathe again.

'We had a few moments of our own during that second half but, for the most part, it was all one-way traffic towards our own goal area. As time went on we packed our area more and more, praying that it would soon be over and we would have victory – and the trophy. Every minute seemed like an hour until, at long last, the final whistle went. Leeds United, holders of the Football League Cup, had become the first British team to take the Inter-Cities Fairs Cup away from the Continentals.'

Billy Bremner remembered well his feelings as he stepped forward to take the trophy from Sir Stanley Rous, president of FIFA.

'It was a moment to savour. For ten years one British team after another had been trying vainly to win this competition. It had always been looked upon as the toughest competition of them all in many ways, because the tournament seemed to spark off trouble and strife of one kind or another nearly every season. British clubs had travelled all over Europe in their efforts to lift this trophy and now, at last, it was Leeds United who had done it.

'If there was one particular hero in that team full of heroes it was probably Gary Sprake. He saved us from a certain goal when he dived to a tremendous free kick, taken by Novak from twenty yards out. Flying through the air, Gary had punched the ball clear with one hand while still in the air. The ball spun high and wide, round a post.'

Billy also had something to say about Leeds United's tactics that night. Always having been labelled a defensive-minded team, critics had been quick to point out their defensive play as a failing.

'Yes, we were called a defensive-minded team – and I'm sure that there has been some justification for being so labelled at times in the past. However, on that night we did no more than any other British team would have done. We played it really tight at the back. I should think that even Manchester United, with all their flair and scoring ability, would have settled for keeping the opposition out rather than risking everything by trying to add to such a slender lead. I admit it was a defensive display, but it was a superb one and it was successful!'

Defensive or not, Leeds supporters had no doubt that their team was one of heroes. They had faced the best that the Hungarians had to offer and had come out on top. Billy himself had this to say about their opponents:

'The man who stood out in the Ferencvaros team was Varga. He twisted and turned like an eel as he tried to penetrate our defensive screen or tried to set up a scoring chance. When it came to shooting, though, he couldn't finish off. We kept Albert contained and he was unable to produce too many threats. I also think our players kept their cool remarkably well, despite quite a bit of rough handling at times, in a game which was tense, to say the least, from the starting whistle onwards.

'After the final we had a celebration in our hotel. Lord Harewood, president of Leeds United and of the Football Association, was at the party with his two sons. They always cheered us on whenever they could at Elland Road and, that night, they had been adding their cheers to those of the small army of supporters who had travelled such a great distance to see us. As the party progressed, we had our usual sing say-or-pay session, in which everyone has to do a turn.

'I was in charge of the session and easily got the players going. I then turned my attention to the press lads, who were a bit reluctant to get up and have a go. Suddenly Don Revie chipped in: "No exceptions Billy – the President next!" You couldn't say no to the boss so, as soon as Gary Sprake ended his not so melodious rendering of "Land of my Fathers", I made the announcement. I simply said, "Gentlemen, pray silence for our president, the Earl of Harewood."

'You could have heard a pin drop, but Lord Harewood was a real sport and did a turn for us. I'm not going to say what it was, except for the fact that he was hardly a Pavarotti, but his turn brought the house down. I do have to say that Lord Harewood's example in joining in with the fun is a classic example of the tremendous team spirit which existed right from the top and down to the bottom at Elland Road.

'On that night, Don Revie had his ambition realized. The Inter-Cities Fairs Cup was the second trophy of the season. When we arrived home there was a tremendous reception from the Leeds fans. We had the League Cup and now we were bringing home the Inter-Cities Fairs Cup. It wasn't a bad haul inside twelve months after all.'

Of course, Leeds United's thoughts turned immediately to the future. They had just had a fair measure of success and now they needed to find other fish to fry, both at home and in Europe.

As holders, Leeds automatically qualified to defend the Inter-Cities Fairs Cup in the 1968/69 season. After beating Standard Liege, Napoli and Hanover, Leeds lost to Ujpesti Dozsa in the fourth round. The release from Europe enabled Bremner and his team-mates to make club history by winning the League championship, the greatest club competition in the world.

On Wednesday 17 September 1969, Leeds played their first European Cup tie – against a team of amateurs from Norway called Lyn Oslo. The first leg was at Elland Road and Leeds were confidently expecting to have little trouble from their amateur opponents. They did not let their fans down either, even though fewer than 26,000 of them turned up for the game. As it happened, Leeds United marked their first-ever European Cup campaign by notching up their highest-ever total of goals and, by the second game, they had created an English scoring record in the tournament.

The line-up for that first game against Lyn Oslo was:

Sprake, Reaney, Cooper, Bremner, Charlton, Hunter, Madeley, Clarke, Jones, Giles, O'Grady. Mick Bates substituted for Giles and, before the European Cup run was over, Mike O'Grady had become a Wolverhampton Wanderers player.

Leeds controlled the game from the start. In fact, they could easily have shown their authority by hitting a dozen goals. There were two occasions when chances were missed – Clarke missed from inside the six-yard box, and Giles didn't even bother with a clear opening from a little further out. Oslo only had two chances, a free kick from Olsen was saved by Gary Sprake as it was streaking towards the corner of the net, and a back-pass by Jack Charlton looked dangerously close to becoming an own goal until it went just wide of the post. The game finished with an incredible 10–0 scoreline, making the return leg a formality.

Leeds were a little slower to dominate in the second leg, although it was obvious from the kick-off which team was going to win. Oslo did not really get into the game at all until the second half and seemed unable to come up with anything to match the skill and firepower of their opponents. The Oslo fans, already expecting another massacre, were clearly happy to show their appreciation of the skilful show that Leeds were putting on. By the end of the game, the Oslo keeper had picked the ball out of the net six more times, giving Leeds an aggregate score of sixteen goals. Leeds United had conquered again and had won new admirers in Europe with their controlled, powerful football, which brought the thing which all fans demanded – goals. Brimming with confidence, Leeds marched forward into the second round of the European Cup where they were drawn to play against Ferencvaros, whom they had beaten in the final of the Fairs Cup in 1968.

As against Lyn Oslo, Leeds got off to a flying start with a Giles goal within ninety seconds. Giles and Jones continually gave the Hungarian defence a real harassing, together with Lorimer, Gray and Reaney. With Gray and Reaney's repeated dashes down the wing, the Ferencvaros defence never really knew where the next danger would materialize. The pattern was set by Gray within a minute of the start of the game when he beat three defenders one after the other, and sped down the left wing. In the muddy conditions, the Hungarians were finding it difficult to turn and combat such moves, despite the fact that they had had fifteen minutes to get used to the pitch before the game. Giles put them to the test when he raced through the mud and passed the ball to Bremner on the edge of the penalty box. Bremner, his back to the goal, flicked the ball with his heel and Giles tore in again and slammed the ball into the net from twelve yards out. The game ended in a 3–0 win for Leeds after a further goal from Giles and another one from Jones.

The return leg in Budapest ended in a similar scoreline and Leeds United were through to the next round. If Ferencvaros had proved to be easier than anticipated, Leeds knew that there was tougher opposition ahead. Their quarter-final opponents turned out to be Standard Liege – the first leg to be played in Belgium. It was a tough nut to crack, but Leeds were up to it and on the night they played like the champions they were. Though Standard made a real fight of it, Leeds were not to be denied and Peter Lorimer scored the only goal of the game, giving them great hopes for the return encounter at Elland Road.

Don Revie was full of praise for the way his players had performed. He said that it was 'one of their most magnificent displays in Europe – a tremendous team performance'. Even Standard Liege's coach, Haus, praised them. He said: 'Leeds United are the strongest team we have ever played in Europe.' Leeds now had only ninety minutes between them and the semi-final of the European Cup.

The return leg at Elland Road was as exciting as the first, with Standard Liege determined to pull back that one-goal deficit. They almost succeeded in the early part of the game too, but Takac's shot hit the side-netting. The only goal of the match came from a penalty awarded when Jones was brought down in the penalty area. Giles was the man entrusted to take the kick and he made no mistake, slotting it home to give Leeds a 2–0 aggregate victory.

It was the only goal of the match and, once again, Leeds had come through without conceding a goal. They had now played for 540 minutes, scored twenty-four goals, and conceded none. Don Revie was jubilant, saying, 'I don't mind who we meet in the semi-finals.'

As fate turned out, the next opponents were the first British team ever to win the European Cup. Celtic, who had won the competition in 1967, were the team that put paid to Leeds United's hopes of winning Europe's major prize. Leeds hadn't come out of their previous encounter with Standard Liege entirely unscathed. Norman Hunter injured a knee which kept him out of several key games. By the time he was back in action, Leeds' chance of the League, European Cup and FA Cup treble had gone out of the window.

The first day of April 1970 was a black one for Leeds United. Everton took over their mantle as League champions, and the team was knocked out of the European Cup by Celtic at Elland Road. For once, Leeds were not the top team; Celtic proved their European pedigree with a display that Leeds United just could not match.

Leeds looked stale. They lacked the fire and fight which had, up to now, always characterized their play in the tournament. They had nowhere near the flair of Celtic on the night. Only days before the match, the Elland Road doctor had said that five of the first-teamers were 'mentally and physically fatigued'. That fatigue showed in the match against Celtic, who could well have won much more convincingly than by the 1–0 scoreline that they took cheerfully back to Glasgow.

The first minute of the game told the whole story. Before the fans even had time to settle down, Celtic were in the lead. The ball came over high, dropped and bounced near the Leeds penalty area. Celtic's Wallace went for the ball and, though he was challenged by Paul Madeley, he succeeded in getting there first. Connelly had come up in support and was there to receive the ball from Wallace. He wasted no time and hammered in a shot, which struck Cooper on the leg and was deflected past the helpless Sprake.

As a rule, United were able to survive such shocks with no trouble, especially if they had time on their side. However, tired and soccer-weary as the players were, this was one time when they seemed unable to fight back. They tried – as they always did – but tired limbs would not respond to equally exhausted brains. The goal, of course, also put great heart into Celtic who immediately carried the play to Leeds.

True to their tradition of never giving up, Leeds tried to stage a comeback in the second half. But they could not really get a grip on a Celtic side that was playing with such assurance and, just when they might have got the break that every team needs, fortune seemed against them as well. The first incident was when Gray emerged from a ruck of players with the ball and hammered in a shot that appeared to have 'goal' written all over it. Williams, in Celtic's goal, had hardly realized that there was a threat to his goal before the ball slammed against the crossbar and made the woodwork shiver.

The other incident where fortune seemed to have deserted Leeds was when Billy Bremner was taken off, suffering from concussion. The game had started without Hunter – which was bad enough – and now, three-quarters of the way through the game, they had lost their indomitable skipper. With Bremner gone, everyone sensed that this was the end of the road for Leeds as far as the first leg went. Bates came on as substitute but the fire had now completely gone from the Leeds side. Bremner, who had hurt his head when he crashed to the ground in the Celtic penalty area, knew nothing of the game for the next twenty minutes or so. After the game, however, he was able to congratulate Celtic on a fine victory.

'Once again,' said Billy Bremner, 'we had been denied the chance of a major success, but we knew that there would be another chance of the European Cup – and we couldn't wait.'

They did have to wait, though, at least for a few years, before they could tackle the European Cup again. However, Bremner and the boys did have another crack at the Inter-Cities Fairs Cup in the 1970/71 season, the last time that it would be contested under that title. Leeds had a successful campaign, too. They sailed through the opening round with a 6–0 aggregate win over Sarpsborg but there was a close call with Dresden in the next round. After the two legs the score was 2–2, but Leeds won on the away-goals rule. Sparta Prague were easier victims in the next round, Leeds winning 6–0 at Elland Road and 3–2 in Prague.

After Vitoria Setubal were beaten 3–2, Leeds faced Liverpool in the semi-final. Billy Bremner scored the only goal of the first leg at Anfield – a goal that proved its worth in the second leg when neither side managed to score. That goal put Leeds into the final, against Juventus.

'We played nearly an hour for nothing when we met in Turin for the first leg,' Billy recalled. 'For fifty-three minutes we played on a pitch which was almost completely under water. The referee abandoned the game and we had to wait for three days before we could play it again. It was a tight game, but we were happy with a 2–2 draw. Back at Elland Road we drew 1–1. It was an exciting game for the supporters who were delighted with the result and our second Inter-Cities win.'

The following season there was an early exit from the competition, which had now become the UEFA Cup. After beating Lierse SK 2–0 away, Leeds had a terrible night in the return leg, losing 4–0 at Elland Road. There was another twist in the story, though, when Leeds played Barcelona in a special play-off between the first and last winners of the Inter-Cities Fairs Cup, to decide who should keep the trophy permanently. Joe Jordan found the net for Leeds, but Barcelona scored twice and went home with the trophy.

The FA Cup holds more than its own special magic; it also holds a key to Europe and, after the parties celebrating Leeds' famous victory in 1972, Billy Bremner eagerly awaited the draw for the European Cup Winners' Cup.

'We knew that we would probably face many of the teams that we had met before, but it felt different because we were in a competition that was completely new to the club.'

The European Cup Winners' Cup did, in fact, throw up a few names that Leeds had not met before – and even one they had never heard of before. They were drawn to play Ankaragucu in the first round and were not even sure which country it was in.

'Our first reaction was, "Who?" Our second reaction was, "Where?" We soon discovered that they were a Turkish side who had won their national cup a couple of times but never anything else. It would have been a big mistake to have dismissed them as being the same as our average non-League sides, because they turned out to be a very strong team indeed. We played them away first of all and they had tremendous support. Joe Jordan scored and we came away with a 1–1 draw – but it had taught us a thing or two about going to Turkey. You can never underestimate any of their teams because they are not only good players, but they also have the odds stacked heavily in their favour by the local conditions and support. Mick Jones finished them off at Elland Road, but we only won 1–0 on the night and 2–1 on aggregate, and they certainly made us work for our result.'

In the second round, Leeds met the more famous Carl Zeiss Jena side but were good value for their 2–0 aggregate success. A competent 0–0 away draw was followed by a very professional 2–0 home victory. In the next round Leeds had to play their first leg at home, a rarity for them in European football. Their opponents were Rapid Bucharest and Leeds took full advantage of being at Elland Road for their first encounter. A 5–0 victory just about guaranteed their passage into the semi-finals, and a 3–1 victory away put the matter beyond any dispute.

'We had to play Hajduk Split in the semi-final and, once again, the home leg was at Elland Road,' said Billy. 'We tried to build up a strong lead again but they played very well and restricted us to just one Joe Jordan goal. That meant that we had to be very careful in the return leg. As it was we held them to a 0–0 draw and went through to the final against AC Milan.'

The game was played in Salonika, in front of 45,000 people, and the preparation for the match had been less than ideal from a Leeds viewpoint.

'It had been a long, hard season. We had been beaten in the FA Cup Final by Sunderland less than a fortnight earlier. We had finished third in the First Division and we had played five League Cup matches as well as our European games. On top of the heavy season of fixtures and the obvious disappointment of missing out in both the League and FA Cups, we were hearing rumours that Don Revie was about to leave us. Allan Clarke and I were suspended, so we had the frustration of watching the game rather than being involved, and then to finish the job there was a major thunderstorm just as the teams came out of the tunnel. The only good thing was that the stadium was fairly new.

'The final score was 1–0 to Milan, but that doesn't tell half the story because we lost to a freak goal after four minutes – and that just about ended the game. The referee gave a free kick for some reason known only to himself. Chiarugi took it, the ball hit one of our players, ricocheted against one of his team-mates, and then deflected against the post before rolling over the line into the goal. It was like watching a pin-ball machine. Milan shut up shop after that and killed the game. They tried to maim a few of our players too. Even the Greek fans in the stands were howling with anger as Mick Jones and Peter Lorimer were both hacked down in the penalty area. Norman Hunter got the same treatment near the end and he had had more than enough. He had a go at Rivera, who had committed the foul, which resulted in he and another Italian, Sogliano, being sent off. A Paul Reaney cross was blatantly handled in the box – but still the referee refused to give a penalty. We began to wonder if his father was from Milan, but then we wondered if he had a father at all. It was one of the most disgraceful performances of refereeing I had ever watched. Knowing me, I would probably not have lasted the match had I been playing!'

Leeds had another tilt at the UEFA Cup the following season. In the first round they defeated Stromgodset Dramman with a 7–2 aggregate, largely thanks to a 6–1 second-leg victory at Elland Road. In the next round they played Hibernian and, after two 0–0 scorelines, the match went to penalties, Leeds winning 5–4. The third round proved to be their downfall because they lost 3–1 in the away leg to Vitoria Setubal after having won 1–0 at home.

'I missed the second leg, so it was frustrating to have to watch again as the boys slipped up,' recalled Billy. 'The only good thing to come out of that competition that season was that we had beaten Hibernian fairly and squarely on penalties. I had always hated the old way of tossing a coin to see who would go through. It had happened to us in the past and I had called successfully but I always felt sorry for the losers. It was almost as if they had been cheated somehow.'

Bremner's final European sortie was in the European Cup of the 1974/75 season, and it proved to be a less than happy ending to his European career. Billy missed the opening-round game against FC Zurich which was won with a 5–3 aggregate. He also missed the first leg of the next round against Ujpesti Dozsa which resulted in a 2–1 away win, but he was back for the return leg and scored one of the goals in a 3–1 success. The third round threw up what appeared to be a tough task against Anderlecht.

'The first leg was at Elland Road and we fancied our chances of getting a decent score. Our supporters were in good voice as usual and, at the end of the match, we were 3–0 to the good. In the return we were expecting Anderlecht to be much stronger. They were not nearly as difficult as we were expecting and our defence were well disciplined to control the game. I managed to grab us a winner and so we made it quite comfortably to the semi-finals where we had to meet Barcelona.'

The Catalan side had not conceded a goal throughout their European Cup campaign that season, but it took Billy Bremner just seven minutes to wreck that record when the two sides met at Elland Road in the first leg. Joe Jordan received a classy pass from Johnny Giles and slipped the ball to Bremner who had found himself some space. He let fly with a shot that had the Spanish goalkeeper clawing at thin air. With less than half an hour to go, Barcelona equalized from a free kick but, ten minutes from the end, Allan Clarke whacked the ball in from close range to restore a deserved lead.

Peter Lorimer scored an early goal in the second leg and that provided a cushion for Leeds. With Bremner as general, the troops kept a tight grip on the game. Barcelona equalized on the night but could not master a Leeds side reduced to ten men following the dismissal of Gordon McQueen. Leeds had reached the final of the European Cup.

'What a night we had in Paris,' said Bremner. 'Bayern Munich were our opponents and we knew that they would be harder than any side we had ever played in our European adventures. We started quite well and, to be honest, we were denied a couple of penalties – and that's an independent view, not mine! We also "scored" through Peter Lorimer. It was a great goal but was disallowed because I was said to have been offside. The fact that I was absolutely nowhere near the play counted for nothing according to the referee. It looked as if the game was heading for extra-time but then there was a mad ten minutes in which the Germans scored twice and finished the game. It ended at 2–0 and I was bitterly disappointed, but worst of all were the problems on the terraces and outside the ground, mostly sparked off by our disallowed goal. There were crowd disturbances in which our supporters were awarded all the blame, and words like "riot" started to be used. The upshot was that we were banned from Europe for four years and I knew then that I would not be playing in any of the European competitions ever again.'

It was a tearful end to European football for Billy Bremner, but among his collection of souvenirs were two Fairs Cup medals – mementoes of the hard work and sheer guts that had brought triumph in Europe.

9

SCOTLAND

One of Billy's favourite subjects was, understandably, Scotland, and we chatted for hours about the pros and cons of Scotland's place in international football. We also talked about his own memories of great games and great moments – and even a few moments that were not quite so great. He was immensely proud to wear his country's shirt and, from our conversations, I always had the impression that he would have loved to have become manager at some stage – although he was always quick to pour praise on the head of current manager Craig Brown.

'He probably has a harder job to do than any manager before him. He has control of every aspect of coaching throughout Scotland and therefore has to keep up with the development of schools soccer, women's soccer, club soccer, the lot. He has to attend overseas seminars and coaching sessions at Largs and any other place where Scottish FA sessions are going. In addition to that, he has to be manager and chief coach of the national team at a time when the Scottish public is crying out for success in a major tournament. That is a lot of pressure for just one man and I take my hat off to Craig for the way that he has handled it all since he took over from Andy Roxburgh. I would love to be Scotland manager, but I'm not sure if I could handle all the other commitments, committee meetings and all the other things which must make life a nightmare at times.

'The Scots have had a variety of team managers over the years. Some have been successful, some have had the breaks going against them. And from what I have gathered, a team spirit has not always been guaranteed. Indeed, I'm told by some players who have worn the dark blue jersey that Scotland has often been her own worst enemy when it came to going for the jackpot and failing to score a hit.'

Billy's own memories of Scottish international football go on from his schools and Under-23 caps to the day he began his career as a senior international.

'I can still vividly remember my first game for Scotland. It was against Spain at Hampden Park on 8 May 1965. We drew 0–0 and among the players in the side that day were Bobby Collins, Denis Law, Alan Gilzean, Billy McNeill, John Greig, Willie Henderson, Bill Brown and Eddie McCreadie, so I was among star company. One incident that I remember was one of the Spaniards throwing a punch at Denis Law. The referee sent him off but the Spaniard was on the ground, allegedly injured. He received treatment for so long that the referee forgot he had dismissed him and let him resume playing! It was a good game as I recall. I was a bit disappointed when we didn't win, especially since I was not picked for the next few games – and I took that personally. Before I made my debut, I travelled and trained with the senior squad. Jock Stein told me not to be impatient as I would soon get my chance. When I was finally picked, I spent a fortune on the phone telling everybody.

'It was the following October when I had a second chance. The team was near enough the same and we were at home to Poland in a World Cup qualifier. They beat us 2–1 and I was devastated. There was a crowd of around 107,000 at Hampden and they were magnificent but we just did not deliver. Mind you, Poland were a very good side and had pulled in some excellent results. The strange thing is, they were hammered 6–1 by Italy a few weeks later and then, a week or two after that, we played Italy at Hampden and beat them 1–0. I didn't expect to play in that game. It wasn't that I had played badly against Poland but, to me, it was all about winning and I thought that if I was not on the winning side, I would not stand much chance of being in the next game. I'm glad I was, though, because it was an amazing experience. Jim Baxter gave the most brilliant individual performance I have ever seen from a Scottish player. To cap it all, in the last minute John Greig let fly with a long-range shot and it flew into the net. Hampden went crazy and the 100,000 members of the Tartan Army there that night would not go home until we came out of the dressing room again to accept their applause. They knew that we had not qualified, but they had enjoyed the victory and the style in which we had played.

'That game against Poland was a vital one for Scotland because whether we qualified for the 1966 World Cup in England hinged on that game. Hampden Park was a cauldron of Scottish fervour that night. We were leading until six minutes from the end when the Poles suddenly struck twice and put us out. After they had got their first goal I remember walking back to the centre circle with Denis Law and saying to him, "Fancy only drawing with this bunch." No sooner had we restarted the game than they went and scored again. It took me a long time to get over that. What made it worse was knowing some of the England players who were going to be competing, and then watching Italy, who we had beaten, doing so badly after they had qualified from our group. We were all sick because we were sure that we could have done better than they did. When England finally won it, a lot of Scots were sicker still. It didn't bother me quite so much because I was happy for Jack Charlton and one or two of the other lads who I knew.

'One of my favourite games came in 1967 when we played against England at Wembley. They had won the World Cup the previous year and had not been beaten since. We were all desperate to bring them down a peg or two. We had a new manager in Bobby Brown and we wanted to do well for him so everything was set for us either to do very well or be sent home with our tails between our legs. I always remember one London newspaper writing, "I do not see it as being a repeat of the 1961 scoreline of 9–3. I cannot see the Scots scoring three goals." That sort of reporting just made us all the more determined to do well.

'As we travelled to Wembley we had encountered thousands of Scots. It was almost as if we were playing at home. Later we discovered that there had been 30,000 of our countrymen at Wembley that day, but they sounded more like 300,000 as we emerged from the tunnel. There had been some nerves in the dressing room, but I will always remember Jim Baxter quietly telling us what he was going to do to humiliate this player or that player. We knew that he meant every word and he almost scared us. One of the surprises the new manager had sprung was giving a debut to our goalkeeper, Ronnie Simpson, who was earning his first cap at the age of thirty-six. The other new cap was Jim McCalliog who was only twenty.

'As soon as the whistle blew to start the game we launched ourselves into the task. Jim Baxter did not waste any time in doing what he had said he was going to do. Once he had the ball he challenged the English defenders to take it away from him and he was like a bullfighter, twisting this way and that with the ball firmly at his feet, as our opponents lunged to try to take it away. They found themselves tackling thin air as Jim pulled the ball out of reach or flicked it to one side at just the right moment. He had said that he was going to take the mickey out of them and he certainly did. He was having the time of his life and he often just stood with one foot on the ball, daring them to come and take it.

'After about ten minutes, Bobby Lennox for Scotland and Big Jack Charlton for England were both injured. Jack went off for about a quarter of an hour and then returned to take up a central attacking position. Later, the newspapers made the excuse that a few knocks had ruined the English game plan. They conveniently forgot to mention that Bobby Lennox carried his injury throughout the game and that Denis Law picked up an ankle injury before half-time that had him limping for the rest of the game. Ironically, we were down to ten men when the first goal came because Tommy Gemmell was stretched out behind the England goal having treatment when it was scored. There was a tremendous roar when the ball hit the back of the net and anyone outside the stadium would have thought that England had scored – but it had been Denis Law who had set the game ablaze. Gordon Banks had saved his first effort, but Denis made no mistake with the rebound.

'We should have rubbed in our advantage then, but we were content to continue playing good football rather than just go for goals. We wanted to show what we could do and Jim Baxter was trying to win a bet. In the dressing room before the game he had bet me how many times he could nutmeg various players. He really tormented the England defenders, so much so that I almost began to feel sorry for them.

England came at us in the second half, determined to stamp their authority on the game. Their pride had been hurt and they had been stung into action. We contained them, though. I sent a shot whistling past the post and then, from the goal-kick, Alan Ball picked up the ball and sent it to Bobby Charlton who let fly with a shot that Ronnie Simpson could only block. The ball went high into the air and when it came down, Charlton headed it towards the goal. Ronnie Simpson dropped on it on the line and there were English protests that the ball had crossed the goal-line. I was right on the spot and it definitely did not, although I would hardly expect any England supporter to believe me.

'The Tartan Army went even crazier when we went 2–0 ahead thanks to a Bobby Lennox goal with just under a quarter of an hour left. England became really desperate then and I remember Alan Ball shouting so much that his voice went even higher than usual and nobody could understand a word that he was saying. Five minutes from the end there was a bit of confusion and Jack Charlton ended a move by scoring. We got going again and Denis Law tried a chip which had "world-class goal" written all over it. However, a world-class save from Gordon Banks stopped it. Jim McCalliog was not to be outdone, though, and a bit of fancy footwork between him and Bobby Lennox ended with Jim putting us 3–1 ahead.

'There was just time for Geoff Hurst to make it 3–2 and that was how it stayed until the end of the game. We had won a sensational victory and the Tartan Army were having their biggest and best party for years. The Wembley pitch was completely covered by dancing Scottish fans. I was dancing with them. When we got back to the dressing room, Jim Baxter worked out how much he had won on his various bets. It came home to all of us that England were world champions and that we were the first team to beat them since they had won the World Cup – and that made us the new world champions as far as we were concerned. Nobody was going to take that moment of glory away from us – and they never have!'

Of course, the Scotland camp's rejoicing was not shared by their hosts. All kinds of reasons were given as to why England had failed on the day. Most of the England players either shrugged off the result or quietly accepted their defeat. Sir Alf Ramsey maintained a cool, politically correct attitude at the press post-mortem, but inside he was seething. He had never been a fan of the Scots and being not just beaten but humiliated by them was more than he could really stand. The celebrations by the Scottish media did little to sweeten his mood and he vowed to gain revenge.

That victory over England was all the sweeter because Scotland had been beaten 4–3 by Alf Ramsey's team at Hampden Park just a couple of months before the 1966 World Cup. Bremner won his fifth full cap in that game, which was a European Championship qualifier. It was another game that Bremner loved to recall, even if it was an England victory.

'We were 2–1 down at half-time but we were not too disappointed because the England forward line of Geoff Hurst, Roger Hunt, Alan Ball and Bobby Charlton were in dazzling form. I think it was during that game that I became convinced that England could win the World Cup. In the second half I witnessed one of the most amazing refereeing decisions ever given on a football field. Bobby Charlton broke to the by-line and chipped the ball over our goalkeeper's head. It looked a simple matter for Geoff Hurst to head home. He launched himself forward just ahead of our defender, Ron McKinnon. Suddenly the ball vanished from in front of Hurst as McKinnon cleared with his hand. Everyone in the ground, on the pitch, on the terraces, in the press box, in fact everywhere, must have seen it happen – except the referee. Geoff Hurst appealed for a penalty and we all expected it to be given but the referee and his linesmen never even looked like giving it. It was one of the worst decisions I have ever seen – though it did make a change to see one go in Scotland's favour. That incident was definitely not one to miss.'

Bremner's next game was in June 1966 when he was in the side which lost 1–0 to Portugal at Hampden Park. After that he played in twelve consecutive Scotland games without defeat. Among those games was a 1–1 draw with Brazil, in which Bremner went head to head with Pele. There followed another 1–1 draw, this time in Cardiff against Wales. A 2–1 victory over Northern Ireland at Hampden came next for Billy, and then that historic defeat of England at Wembley. Wales were the next victims, before a 1–1 draw with England at Hampden and then a tremendous 1–0 victory over Denmark in Copenhagen.

His first goal for Scotland came during that great sequence, in November 1968 when Austria were visitors to Hampden Park for a World Cup qualifier. It was an important game for both sides because West Germany were in the same group and nobody doubted that they would make it to Mexico.

'There was another big crowd at Hampden,' said Billy. 'As usual, the Tartan Army was brilliant and was willing us on to win. They were stunned into silence when Austria scored after just two minutes. They didn't stay quiet for long, though, and the Hampden roar was ringing in our ears when Denis Law scored from a corner five minutes later. We nearly scored again a few minutes further on when I slipped the ball to Charlie Cooke and he hit the crossbar. About a quarter of an hour before the end, we were attacking and the ball fell in the middle of a crowd of players in front of the goal. Everyone aimed a kick at it and it happened to be my foot that connected. The ball went over the line and we were 2–1 ahead. It stayed that way too so I was quite pleased with my first goal for Scotland.'

What Billy Bremner failed to mention was that the game not

only marked his first goal for Scotland, but also he was made captain for the second time. He had certainly led by example. The Scots had played with a 4–2–4 formation, but with the way Bremner played it seemed more like 5–3–5.

By the time that he was made captain, Bremner had played for two Scotland managers. Jock Stein had given him his debut while he was in charge, but then Bobby Brown had taken over, and as part of his rebuilding plans he asked Bremner to take over the captaincy for the match in Copenhagen.

'It didn't really sink in the first time when we played Denmark, although I was happy enough to start with a victory. Then, when we played Austria at Hampden and I looked at the match programme and saw my photograph with the caption "Billy Bremner, captain of Scotland", I suddenly realized just what this honour meant. It made me feel deeply proud and confident. I promised myself, there and then, that I would do my best to follow in the footsteps of all those great Scotland captains who had gone before me.

'That is why I gave it everything in the next game at home to Austria. I wanted to show everyone that I really understood my responsibilities. Bobby Brown had told me before the game that once we were on the field, if I felt that there was something to be done, I must be prepared to take matters into my own hands. There was something to be done all right when Austria took the lead. Then, later in the game, I knew that a draw was no good to us and so we turned up the pressure even more and that is when I got the winner. All I saw was the ball and about a dozen boots aimed at it. Mine made contact just before one of those other boots landed on my leg.'

Denis Law recalled Bremner's captaincy.

'He was a natural leader. He kept everyone on their toes even when he wasn't captain, so it was just a question of making it official. I've never known anyone with so much energy. I don't ever remember seeing him take a breather. You always got the impression that if there was a pause in the game he would be likely to start a training session. He would talk to you and keep driving you throughout the game. Nobody could ever point the finger at him because he always gave everything in every game he played. If Billy Bremner said "run", you ran.'

Despite taking Cyprus apart to the tune of 8–0 at Hampden Park in May 1969, Scotland failed to qualify for the 1970 World Cup. They also sat out the 1972 European Championship, although they had excellent victories over Portugal and Belgium in the qualifiers.

Bremner was desperate to play in at least one of these finals tournaments, and time was inexorably passing away. Every failure meant at least another two years of waiting before another chance came along.

'There is not a footballer in existence who does not want to play for his country in the World Cup tournament,' said Bremner. 'In many ways it is worse if you get close but then don't make it. I was determined that I would play in one of these major tournaments – but it was the World Cup that I really wanted desperately. I had this burning ambition.'

It was an ambition that was destined to be fulfilled.

10

THE WORLD CUP

By 1974 Scotland had not appeared in a World Cup finals tournament since 1958, when they finished bottom of a group that also included France, Yugoslavia and Paraguay. As the new millennium approaches, Scotland have restored their pride by missing only one of the last seven World Cups. That run began, of course, when Billy Bremner was captain. It was no simple passage, however, for along the way there were both triumphs and traumas – with Billy in the thick of all of them.

Bobby Brown had left the manager's job in the summer of 1971 and Tommy Docherty had taken over, first of all as caretaker-manager and then as the real thing. The World Cup draw for qualifying groups was quite kind to Scotland as they were in a group with only two other countries, Denmark and Czechoslovakia. Docherty started the job of qualifying but it was Willie Ormond who finished it when Docherty left to become manager of Manchester United.

With Docherty at the helm, Bremner continued to flourish as captain of the national side. At the same time there had been a major change at the headquarters of the Scottish Football Association. Previous managers had been forced to pick their teams in collaboration with a selection committee but Docherty had become Scotland's first go-it-alone manager. Bremner welcomed the change of policy.

'It was long overdue. The less we had to do with committees the more likely we were to be successful. How could one man be expected to run things if he wasn't being left alone to do it?

I don't know how the previous managers had been able to stand it. I know that Bobby Brown had continual problems because of the club-versus-country situations. I don't ever remember Leeds refusing to allow me to go – but Liverpool and Manchester United had both declined to release their players for internationals and that had tied the Scotland manager's arms behind his back. Tommy Docherty was able to sort out that sort of thing without having to talk to a committee for their approval.

'Tommy Docherty also brought in a different approach. He wanted us to hit hard, whether it was in the tackle or taking a shot. He made wholesale changes to the squad and I think there was only Peter Lorimer, apart from myself, who had been in the nucleus of the side that had tried for the previous World Cup. Our first game against Denmark was in Copenhagen and the Doc told us not to think in terms of them being part-timers. They were the enemy as far as he was concerned and he encouraged us not to take prisoners. We didn't. We beat them 4–1 and it could have been more. I don't suppose it was very pretty to watch and I don't think that the Danes took too kindly to the treatment they received, but that win gave us our first victory overseas for nearly four years, and it meant that we had got off to a flying start in our attempt to get to West Germany for the 1974 World Cup.'

The return match of that group was played a month later in mid-November 1972 at Hampden Park.

'We beat them 2–0, and I think they had decided to try to play us at our own game. They tried to tackle hard but really we were well used to that. The game became a bit physical and reached boiling point when Peter Lorimer was hacked from behind for the umpteenth time. He swung a fist at his assailant and they were both sent off. The game was not so much a football match as a revenge mission on the part of the Danes. Had we been able to play some decent football we would have had a more convincing scoreline than just 2–0. There were some good points, though. Our first goal came after just two minutes and it was the very first international goal scored by a guy by the name of Kenny Dalglish. Another point was that Denmark used a substitute who was a very good player indeed and who went on to become a big star. Finn Laudrup was his name and not only was he a top-class player but he had two sons, Michael and Brian, who have since become world-class players. The most important point of all, though, was that we had won our first two games and were well on our way to the World Cup finals.

'It was a blow to us when Tommy Docherty resigned soon afterwards. We couldn't blame him for taking up the Manchester United job, but we didn't want to lose our manager just as things were going so well. Willie Ormond took over and was a completely different sort of character. The Doc was rough and ready, Willie was much quieter and almost seemed to be apologizing for being there.'

Bremner was also frustrated by the results of the new manager's first games in charge – thankfully none of them with a World Cup place at stake.

'Our first game with Willie was a special SFA Centenary game against England at Hampden. It turned out to be a huge embarrassment as we were thumped 5–0 in our own backyard. It was supposed to be our party but there were no celebrations in our dressing room afterwards. I wanted the ground to swallow me up. The new manager changed everything that Tommy Docherty had put in place. I could understand that, in the long term, he wanted things to be his way – but the short-term result was that we were all over the place and England just picked us off. I cannot stand to see that scoreline in the record books. It makes me cringe every time I accidentally come across it.'

Things did get better, but it took a little time. After the centenary game, Bremner skippered the side to four more consecutive defeats, two of them at Hampden Park. Northern Ireland won 2–1, England then beat the Scots 1–0 at Wembley, a trip to Berne resulted in a 1–0 defeat by Switzerland, and then Brazil also won 1–0 at Hampden. It was not the ideal preparation for the next World Cup game against Czechoslovakia at

Hampden in September 1973 – some ten months after the successes against Denmark.

'It was another physical game,' recalled Billy. 'The Czechs started it. They came to defend at all costs and within the first few minutes both Kenny Dalglish and Tommy Hutchison, who was making his debut, were felled harshly. Someone also took my legs away and got booked for it. I then tackled someone else a bit hard just to let them know that we would not be standing for that sort of nonsense. Unfortunately he had to go off and the Czechs used their first substitute. That was the tone of the game and we had only been playing for about twenty minutes. We were a bit shocked when the Czechs scored just after the half-hour. They hadn't even looked like attacking, let alone scoring. We went level about five minutes before half-time when Jim Holton got on the end of a Denis Law corner and put it home.

'I was clattered again in the second half and that was another Czech booked. We liked to play it hard but we played it as a man's game, hard but fair. The Czechs liked to play it hard and unfair but we refused to be drawn into a battle that distracted us from winning the game. When I hit the post about halfway through the second half, the ball whipped across the face of the goal before it was punted back in and Joe Jordan, my Leeds team-mate, headed it home. We were in front and we stayed in front. At the end of the game we knew that we had done enough to qualify for the World Cup and Hampden went crazy. Willie Ormond found himself being carried shoulder-high around the ground and the whole of Scotland celebrated.

'I missed the return match because of an ankle injury. The press over there made a big deal of that and said I was duck-ing out of the game because of cowardice. I've been called a few things but I don't think I have ever been branded as a coward either before or since. If it had not been so ridiculous I would have felt insulted, but it was too stupid to warrant a response of any sort. Scotland were ordered to cruise through the game to avoid unnecessary injuries or unpleasantness and we lost 1–0 when the Czechs were awarded a penalty for hand-ball. The result did not matter to us because we had already qualified. The shock news to us was that England had not made it. They failed to beat Poland at Wembley and that was them out of the World Cup. I felt sorry for some of the England guys I knew but it was awful hard not to smile!'

Scottish fans became more and more excited as the weeks ticked away before the World Cup tournament in West Germany. The draw put their country in the same group as Brazil, Yugoslavia and Zaire. It was a mixed bag with defeat by Brazil a likely outcome, anything less than victory over Zaire unthinkable, and a showdown with Yugoslavia as the likely route to the second phase. There were a few friendly matches to be played as part of the build-up to the tournament and, with such mixed results as victories over England and Norway and defeat at home by Northern Ireland, it was difficult to assess Scotland's chances. There was, however, an incident in Norway which could have wrecked Bremner's chances of playing in the World Cup tournament of which he had dreamed so often.

A group of travelling journalists were drinking in a student bar around midnight when, suddenly, Jimmy Johnstone and Billy Bremner turned up. After the initial shock of seeing two of Scotland's leading players openly flaunting a curfew, the party was treated to a bout of community singing, led by the two soccer stars. The party was in full swing when manager Willie Ormond suddenly arrived. He looked at them, said nothing, then turned away and left. A few moments later Dr Fitzsimmons, the SFA doctor, arrived and took the two players away.

'I think everyone was waiting for the balloon to go up,' said Bremner. 'It was one of those things. Neither of us could sleep because the rooms were so bad. We decided to go for a walk and bumped into the journalists, most of whom we knew. We weren't out getting drunk or anything like that. We just couldn't rest. We explained this to the manager. Understandably he wasn't very pleased, but he didn't disagree with what we said about the poor sleeping arrangements. He was very good about it really because he could have gone off the deep end and sent us both back home. However, Willie Ormond was not one for locking up his players. He trusted them to know what was best for themselves and, even though the press was having a field day with Jimmy and myself being nominated for public hanging when we got back home, he took a more lenient view. We thought that he might well have to make examples of us and both Jimmy and I were resigned to being sent back, but Willie Ormond decided not to bow to the pressure of the press and it was announced through the SFA that we would be staying with the squad. The press was mixed in their reaction. I think that what annoyed Jimmy and myself the most was the fact that some of those who had been happy to join in with the singing were the loudest in calling for us both to be expelled.'

The action moved on to Germany and there were the usual press conferences as the first game approached. Jock Stein was in West Germany, working as a TV pundit for the BBC. He attended a press conference at which Bremner was the Scotland representative. Bremner seemed rather subdued. Anyone who did not know him better might even have thought that he had lost interest. Gradually it was coaxed out of him that he did not like the way that the press was treating Scotland, writing them off almost, before they even had a chance to prove themselves. He was still stung by the treatment his so-called pals in the media had given him and Jimmy Johnstone over the Oslo affair, and also reports of excessive drinking in Belgium for the previous warm-up game. Bremner also hinted that he felt the management had something to answer for in allowing things to get to such a state. It was then that Jock Stein stepped in.

'He was sitting facing me, just a couple of feet away,' recalled Bremner. 'He suddenly clenched his fist and held it up before him and told me that, if anybody could influence the players into performing for pride, it was me, and that I should stop moaning and get on with proving the press boys to be exactly what I thought they were. He told me that the players held all the answers themselves and that I was the guy to motivate them and, as Jock put it, "stick it right up the press". He told me to take the players out there and show everyone what we were made of. It was probably the best team talk I had had in years. He was right. It may not have been the most ideal place to say it, but he was right.'

Scotland did go out and prove their point. They still came in for criticism for not beating Zaire by a bigger margin than the final score of 2–0, but it was their first-ever victory in a World Cup finals tournament and nobody was going to take that away from them.

'You just can't please everyone,' Bremner said later. 'If we had scored a hatful against Zaire we would have been branded as bullies. If we didn't we would be branded as inadequate. As it was, we saw what they were made of, scored two goals, and then sat back with the notion that we still had our toughest two games to come and we didn't want injuries or suspensions spoiling our chances. Zaire had a guy booked after he gave me a good kicking so they were not above putting their weight about. It was a good game and we were all friends at the end of it. We had the usual criticism for our performance, but to gain your first World Cup win, with something left in reserve, was good enough for us.

'We were over-cautious when we played Brazil four days later. We paid them far too much respect for the first half before realizing that they were human just like we were and that they made mistakes like the rest of us. We gradually grew in confidence and at half-time when we heard that Yugoslavia were beating Zaire 6–0 we knew that we really had to go for it in the second half. The Tartan Army were terrific and backed us all the way. We put a lot of pressure on the Brazilians and we were desperately close to scoring when the ball came off my shins and rebounded just inches the wrong side of the post when the goalkeeper was stranded. We were so very close but we just could not break them down. At the end it was 0–0 and we knew that we had it all to do against Yugoslavia. I could not stop thinking about that nearly goal. We had been just two inches away from a famous victory.

'We knew that we had to beat Yugoslavia to get through the group. They had beaten Zaire 9–0 and we doubted that Brazil would fail to beat them in their final group match, so we simply had to get the right result against Yugoslavia. There were all kinds of statistics being mentioned in the press. It was said that Yugoslavia had never beaten Scotland. We were reminded that, in 1958, the two teams had played each other at exactly the same stage and had drawn 1–1 – which meant that Yugoslavia had gone on to the next stage while Scotland had returned home. The speculation went on and on but we just concentrated on preparations for the game.

'It was a hot, energy-sapping day, but we knew that it was do or die for us so we set the pace. The game was a tough one and there were plenty of incidents but, with ten minutes to go, it was still 0–0. We had heard that Brazil were in the lead but, if they did not score again, we would have a better goal difference and would go through. Then the Yugoslavs scored and that wrecked everything – or so it seemed. We pushed even harder and, with two minutes left, Joe Jordan headed a goal which put us back on level terms. We felt that we were going to make it and when the final whistle went we were ready to celebrate getting through the group stage. Then the scoreboard flashed the result from the other match. Brazil had won 3–0 and therefore had a better goal difference. It was 1958 all over again. Zaire were bottom of the group with no points while the rest of us had four each. Yugoslavia were top, Brazil were second and we were third. Brazil had scored three and conceded none; we had also scored three but had conceded one. If only we had been more ruthless against Zaire. If only that goal had gone in against Brazil. You think of things like that for weeks afterwards, but it doesn't change anything. We had been, but we had not conquered.'

Bremner was to play just three more games for Scotland. He had already passed the fifty-cap mark which meant that he was to become a member of the exclusive club of Scotland internationals whose portrait would be placed in the Scottish Football Association's Hall of Fame. His international career had been star-studded with more victories than defeats and a catalogue of superb performances. Yet it all came to a less than glittering end.

Scotland were in Denmark for a European Championship qualifying match in September 1975. They won the game 1–0, but there was supposed trouble in a nightclub over a bill. Billy was involved along with Arthur Graham, Willie Young, Pat McCluskey and Joe Harper. Nobody knew exactly what had happened but it emerged that there had been an argument and punches had been thrown.

Within a few days, the Scottish Football Association had taken, what they saw, as the right action. They banned each of the five players for life. Billy Bremner was devastated. To everyone else, it seemed incredible that a man could play for his country so many times, lead them to an historic World Cup victory, yet be dismissed so easily from the international scene.

Billy never really liked to talk about it. At the time he simply said, 'It was all based on rumour and it was all nonsense. There was no row in a club, no fight and no trouble about a bill. Anyway, what we do in our spare time has nothing to do with anyone else. I was staggered by the SFA decision. They came to their conclusions by listening to what other people thought happened, not the facts.'

Much later he told me, 'It was all a storm in a teacup. Of course there was an incident, but it was nothing like what was reported and I think we were all victims of gross exaggeration by the media and officials who wanted to be able to control us and couldn't. If it had happened about twenty years later it would hardly have been mentioned. The situation simply involved a small group of young Scottish guys who objected to being ripped off. I know there was probably an over-reaction but the circumstances were most definitely mitigating. I have always loved my country and if anyone thinks that I would bring it into disrepute off the pitch after all that I have tried to do on it, they want to go and see a psychiatrist.'

It was the end of his international career and Leeds United also gave him something of a talking to, even though he continued to protest his innocence – and he did so for as long as he lived. For their part, the Scottish Football Association appeared to forgive, but not to forget. His portrait continued to hang in the Hall of Fame, but he was never encouraged to apply for the Scotland manager's job when it became vacant. It was also noticeable that no representative of the Scottish Football Association attended Billy's funeral.

An official spokesperson said, after the event, 'We understood from the media that the funeral was for family and close friends, so we left it at that.' Billy would have found it quite ironic that the SFA took their cue from the media.

The current Scotland boss, Craig Brown, called for an area of the new-look Hampden Park to be named after Bremner. He said:

'Billy Bremner was one of the greatest captains and players that this country has ever had, and the memory of all that he stood for on the pitch should not be allowed to pass away. I'm sure that at least a part of Hampden could be named after him, perhaps the fitness and rehabilitation centre. That would seem very appropriate to me.'

There were, and still are, many members of the Tartan Army who would agree with him. Without any shadow of a doubt, Billy Bremner left the dressing room for every international game fully prepared to die for his country.

Even after achieving his personal ambition of playing in the World Cup, Bremner lost none of his ambition for his country. Alex Smith remembered a conversation with Billy not long before he died.

'We were talking about Scotland's chances and he was very upbeat about them. He admired the modern squad and Craig Brown, and I knew that if he had been alive he would have obtained a ticket or two and joined the Tartan Army in France.'

On 8 May 1965 Billy Bremner stood proudly at attention in a

Scotland shirt as he made his debut at senior level for his country. Ten years later he took his final bow with a victory in Denmark. Despite winning so many caps, none of his pride or passion ever diminished. He didn't just play for Scotland – he was Scotland.

11

LEEDS TO HULL

With the excitement of the World Cup over it was back to business for Billy Bremner and Leeds United. As reigning League champions, Leeds had much to live up to and there was the added attraction of battling again for the European Cup. However, before the season started there was also the little matter of meeting Liverpool at Wembley in the FA Charity Shield. The players also had to get used to a new manager. Brian Clough, previously a fierce critic of the Leeds style of play, was the surprise choice to replace Don Revie, who had now gone on to his new challenge in the England hot seat. Many supporters were up in arms about the choice because of things that Clough had said about Leeds, and indeed about Bremner, in the past. He once said, 'I despised what they stood for, systematically putting referees under intolerable pressure with their violent behaviour, both physical and verbal, their over-reactions, and the unsavoury spectacle of Billy Bremner running alongside the harassed referee constantly yelling in his ear.' Those sort of statements were hardly likely to endear him to the Leeds United faithful.

'We were all a bit shocked when we heard the news that Clough had got the job,' said Bremner. 'We couldn't imagine why he would want it after all the things that had been said in the past. He didn't stay very long because he knew what a thankless task he had in trying to change what had become a very successful family unit at Elland Road.'

It was Clough, however, who performed the duty of leading

Leeds United out at Wembley Stadium alongside Bill Shankly. Shankly was leading Liverpool out even though he had already resigned as manager at Anfield. It was an afternoon of token gestures – and some not quite so token . . .

The game was being televised live for the first time and should have been the showpiece to herald the start of the new season. But the rivalry between the two clubs manifested itself in late tackles and niggles, reaching boiling point in the second half when Kevin Keegan, who had been sent off in a friendly the week before, clashed with Bremner.

'I took one knock too many and I just lost it,' said Keegan. 'No complaints about being sent off or the consequences. I was just upset that I had embarrassed Bill Shankly on his farewell.'

The pair had come to blows and were immediately dismissed. As they went off together they both stripped off their shirts, angrily it seemed, and that had the Football Association's white-collar brigade almost choking on their gin and tonics.

'I don't know why we took our shirts off. Neither of us could explain it,' said Keegan later. 'The affair was over as soon as it had started as far as we were both concerned. There were no harsh words. We met many times in the years that followed and we never discussed it again.'

The game itself ended in a 1–1 draw and Liverpool were awarded the match after a penalty shoot-out in which Leeds goalie David Harvey sent the ball flying over the crossbar when it was his turn to shoot. The game, of course, became of secondary importance compared to the yards of newsprint that were expended on every aspect of the Keegan–Bremner affair.

They were both fined £500 and banned until the end of September, which meant missing quite a few games since several fixtures are crammed into the beginning of a season. Bremner never wasted his time by dwelling on such incidents.

'It was one of those things,' he said. 'A momentary flare-up that just happened to be in front of the television cameras and invited guests. Football is a physical game, there is no time for pleasantries during a match. Those come much later when you are shaking hands and congratulating each other or asking about each other's injuries. As for taking our shirts off, it was a hot day and we were both annoyed, which made it worse. If you are hot, you take your shirt off, if you are upset about something, you are inclined to do it a little aggressively. We are only human and we do things like that. We didn't throw our shirts at each other or anything like that. I think it was another case of the Football Association trying to appease their own image of themselves rather than handle a moment of madness in a more humane way.'

Of course, this was not Billy Bremner's only well-publicized clash with another player. The all-time classic photograph of him protesting his innocence as Dave Mackay threatens him has appeared in newspapers, books and magazines all over the world. Dave Mackay explained what happened.

'I fouled wee Billy and he got up and kicked me, so I lost my cool and grabbed hold of him. The truth is I was scared and I was bluffing my way out of the situation. I had just returned after an eighteen-month lay-off with a leg break, and when Billy kicked me it was like a warning that there were further reprisals on the way so, in a way, I was protecting myself. I suppose it was inevitable that when you'd put two tough Scots against each other there was bound to be a showdown.

'What many people don't know is that we went to the nearest bar after the game and had a good drink together. We remained good friends ever after.'

Bremner took a similar view of the incident.

'Dave Mackay thought I was going to have a go and he grabbed hold of me first. I was actually innocent. I had made my point and that was the end of it, but I think he believed that I was going to give him and everyone else a good kicking. We had a laugh about it later and, to be honest, I love that photograph because it shows me with one of my all-time heroes.'

When the 1974/75 League season got under way, Bremner played in the very first game which was a surprise 3–0 defeat at Stoke. He then missed the following fourteen First Division games, partly because of his ban but also because of an injury sustained in his comeback game, a League Cup tie against Bury. There were other problems for Leeds as Clough was sacked after just forty-four days as manager of the club. It was suggested that he was removed because of player power. Billy Bremner remembered the difficulties of that time.

'The players didn't dispense with Clough's services, the board did. There is no doubt that he was a very good manager and he has had success after success, but he was not for Leeds United – not at that time. His style of management just would not work with the Leeds players and, yes, we did have our moans and groans about the situation. We didn't force him out but we aired our views to each other and, if we were asked, to members of the board. We were all interested in the future of Leeds United and we knew that the only way to continue our successful run under Don Revie was to keep the same style of management and the same style of play. The board members took the final decision, not us. There was a lot of controversy at the time and all we wanted to do was to get on with our jobs.'

Although still under suspension, Bremner was involved in picking the side for the first game after Clough's departure. He, assistant manager Maurice Lindley, and Syd Owen selected the team to play away to Burnley but made few changes, the only notable omission being John O'Hare – a Clough signing. The Burnley trip ended in defeat and meant that Leeds had secured only one victory in their opening seven First Division fixtures. A 5–1 home win over Sheffield United helped a little but form was generally a hit-and-miss affair during the following weeks. Following a 1–0 home defeat, Leeds found themselves at their lowest ebb for ten years. They had won just four of their fifteen games and had suffered eight defeats, twice as many as in the whole of the previous season. They were in nineteenth place and new manager Jimmy Armfield was beginning to age. However, there was about to be a dramatic change with the return of Billy Bremner to the team.

'I came back against Coventry in an away game. The club had not yet had an away win that season and for me it was the end of a very frustrating time. I was determined that we should win. Sitting on the sidelines had been nothing short of agony, but now I had the chance actually to be doing something about the mess we were in.'

John O'Hare was in the side for his sixth and final appearance for Leeds and he wasted little time in getting on the scoresheet. When Peter Hindley put through his own goal to make it 2–0, the writing was on the wall for Coventry and the Leeds dressing room was back to normal. Bremner scored a third in the second half and Leeds finished 3–1 winners and thus secured a desperately needed victory. SuperBrock was back!

Leeds then went four games unbeaten. They drew against Middlesbrough, and then beat Chelsea, Carlisle and Tottenham. There were more defeats to follow, but there were more victories too, and Leeds finished the season in ninth place, eight points behind the ultimate champions, Derby County, managed by Dave Mackay.

'We were not too disappointed with that,' said Bremner. 'We had come through all kinds of problems at the start of the season and we had also reached the European Cup Final. I don't think that finishing ninth with all that to contend with was anything to be depressed about. We could have done better perhaps, but equally we might have done a lot worse.'

The following season Leeds had Don Howe as assistant to Jimmy Armfield and results were better. There was a cloud hanging over the club, though, because of their failure in the European Cup Final and the crowd trouble which saw them banned from European competition for four years. The season started with a 2–1 victory at Aston Villa and, after the first three games, Leeds had won two and drawn one. Then they were shaken by a 3–0 home defeat by Liverpool. As always, Billy Bremner played his part in rallying his troops and the Leeds championship challenge became stronger as the season wore on.

In the middle of January 1976 Leeds were second in the table. Bremner was then forced to miss seven games, a period during which the side won one, drew three and lost three, slipping down to fifth place. There had been a run of four consecutive victories beforehand. Bremner returned in the middle of March to a 3–2 defeat at Manchester United in which he scored and inspired his team to frighten the life out of the Manchester side which had been 2–0 ahead at half-time. The near-60,000 Old Trafford crowd was stunned as Leeds staged one of the most dramatic fight-backs ever seen at the ground. The third Manchester goal proved to be one too many for Leeds but suddenly they had found form and a sense of direction again. The next four games all resulted in victories. One of those wins was a 3–0 home success over Arsenal. It did not seem so significant at the time that Allan Clarke scored two and his pal Billy Bremner the other, but it was to be Bremner's last goal for Leeds United.

However, the Bremner influence had lost none of its importance in the Leeds side and the final placing in the table was fifth, a clear improvement. But Bremner was now approaching his thirty-fourth birthday after having been the battery charger for Leeds for sixteen years. How much longer could he keep going? How could Leeds break out of their dependence on him? The answers to those questions came the following season.

After missing the first two games of the new season, Bremner returned to the side for an away match at Coventry. It was a bit like history repeating itself except that this time the scoreline was in the home side's favour, Coventry winning 4–2. Derby were then beaten before Tottenham won 1–0 at White Hart Lane. On 18 September 1976, Leeds were at home to Newcastle and for Billy Bremner it was to be one of the most significant games of his entire career. It was to be his 587th and final League appearance for Leeds United. The score was 2–2, all the goals coming in the second half. When the game ended Billy waved to the crowd before disappearing down the tunnel, not knowing that he had just made his farewell performance.

'It was a few days later that John Kaye, the Hull City manager, came in for me,' recalled Billy. 'I talked it over with everyone and finally agreed to the transfer. I knew that my days at Leeds were likely to be numbered, although I had hoped to be playing again throughout that season. Leeds did well out of the deal because they sold me for £25,000. I had cost them nothing when they had signed me as a boy. After I had signed the contract I was all smiles, but inside I felt numb. There was a lump in my throat and I felt near to tears. It all seemed so unreal. All my footballing life I had been at Elland Road and yet here I was leaving the place. Not only that, I was expected to look happy about it. Leeds had been my life. I said all the right things to the press and I did look forward to a new challenge at Hull, which I had always considered to be a good club. But I was having to say goodbye to something which seemed always to have been there – I was leaving home.'

When Billy Bremner told me that, it was a good many years later and yet the pain of taking that decision still showed in his face. If the Leeds fans had loved him it was certainly no more than the feelings that he had for them and the club they supported. When a vast crowd turned up at Elland Road for his testimonial in 1974, he was quite taken aback by the show of respect, admiration and affection. The game earned him £40,000 – a week's wages for some of today's players, although it was considered to be quite a sum in those days. In the programme for that celebration game he put into perspective the then controversy over players' supposed high salaries.

'To a certain extent football is still white slavery. We are entertainers, playing to packed galleries every Saturday and often in between. People flock from all corners of the country to see us perform, to see what it is that makes us stand out from the crowd. But our earnings are unrelated to our crowd-pulling power ... It makes me smile when people talk about big-money footballers.'

John Kaye was obviously delighted at capturing such a legend for Hull City. He had high hopes that Bremner could do for Hull City what he had done for Leeds United.

'I've brought him here to inspire my side to promotion,' he said. It was a tall order. Inspiration is one thing, the ability of those to be inspired is quite another. Nevertheless, there was inspiration of a sort when Billy Bremner made his debut as a Tiger. Hull were at home to Nottingham Forest, who were four places above Hull in seventh place in Division Two. A crowd of 16,096, more than twice the previous season's average, turned up to see the new signing in action. They were not disappointed. Not only did Billy motivate Hull to victory, but he scored the only goal of the game. It was a dream debut.

What followed was a catalogue of inconsistency. Having reached fifth place in the table, Hull could not keep up the momentum and started to slip down again – eventually settling for a mid-table position. Bremner had a few niggling injuries which meant that he missed several important games, including a 4–0 defeat at Chelsea at the end of the season which killed off any chance of Hull creeping into a top-ten placing in the Second Division.

The 1977/78 season was not a good one. Hull started fairly well, but could not maintain their encouraging form. In October, John Kaye left the club and there was some talk that Bremner might take over as manager, but it was Bobby Collins who was given the job.

'It was great to be working with Bobby again, but we both knew that there was more to Hull's problems than a change of face and tactics would solve. There was simply not the strength or quality of squad, or even the means with which to buy in top players. Bobby gave it a good try but very little changed and Bobby was never a man to waste his time. He left in February after just four months.'

Bremner was in and out of the side, finding it more difficult to overcome minor injuries which had previously meant nothing to him. Ken Houghton had become caretaker manager and, in April 1978, he was confirmed as the man to take over permanently. He did not have the best of baptisms as Hull lost their last five games and finished bottom of the Second Division.

Bremner had missed the last three games of the season because of his aches and pains and was finally forced to admit that his serious playing days were over. He had made more than 900 first-class appearances.

'It was time to move on,' said Billy. 'There was nothing more that I could do for Hull or anyone else as a player at that stage. I didn't even want to play unless I was capable of giving of my very best and I was well aware that I just could not do that week in and week out any more. I had enjoyed my couple of seasons at Hull, even though the results were not all that we would have liked. I could probably have gone and played for someone else for a season or two, but there was no real point. I would have felt as if I were cheating them and the supporters if I wasn't the same Billy Bremner, and I didn't want to do that. The game had been very good to me and I did not want to be not good in return. It was high time that I put my boots away and went in search of a different job. I wanted it to be in football, but I also wanted time in which to think. I did not want to rush into anything.'

Bremner took time out to enjoy his family. There were trips back to Scotland as always and the telephone rang quite often with suggestions, requests for interviews, and open offers to join various clubs as player-coach. However, Bremner was a family man and he did not want to pull up the anchor suddenly and drift off in some direction that would take him away from home all the time. If he was going to take a job, it would have to be somewhere near by, or he would simply stay out of it altogether and find something entirely different to occupy his time.

'We all knew that he would not be able to stay away from football,' said his wife Vicky. 'It was a question of when rather than if. We all held our breath and waited for him to come across something that appealed to him. We couldn't really see him running a corner shop somewhere. For him, football had always been the answer, even as a child, and he had lost none of his appetite for the game. We all knew that, instead of ending his career, he was probably just about to start a whole new part of it.'

She was absolutely right, of course. Eventually the phone

did ring with the right message and, once again, Billy Bremner was on his toes in search of triumph.

That phone call did not come for some months, however, and, when the new season started in August 1978, Billy Bremner found that he was not involved, for the first time since he had travelled south of the border.

'I did some interviews, and a few radio and television programmes, but they were almost synthetic. I kept looking at the dates on the newspapers and thinking that it was time for pre-season training, or the usual dates for those pre-season friendlies. When the season actually started and the day of the big kick-off arrived, it was dreadful I can tell you. It made you feel as if you were a hundred years old and that you had been put out to pasture.

'As the time approached 3 p.m. I mentally went through every detail of the normal pre-match routine. I must have been really awful to live with at that time. It is not a nice feeling to realize that, despite everything, life goes on without you.'

Well, life did go on – but for many it was not the same without Billy Bremner.

12

DONCASTER'S BOSS

Having 'retired' from playing, Billy Bremner was looking for a new challenge within the game when the chance of becoming manager of Doncaster Rovers presented itself in November 1978. Stan Anderson had been in charge for three years but had decided to call it a day and take up another opportunity as assistant manager at Bolton. When Billy took over, Doncaster were in the throes of their customary struggles, a real shame for the supporters who were trying to celebrate the club's centenary.

Bremner's reign began positively when his new side beat Rochdale 1–0 at home in his first League game in charge. It turned out to be a false start as the side slumped to two defeats, rose to two victories, and then fell to an horrendous 7–1 mauling at Bournemouth.

'I knew that Donny had not been in good shape for some time, but it was difficult to know just where to start because they were so inconsistent. There were players who looked really on course for promotion one week, and then relegation the next. Even after Bournemouth hammered us so heavily, we went out and won the next three games and went up into mid-table. It was hard to keep up with.'

Having crept up the table, Doncaster then slid back down again and finished the season in twenty-second place. A 4–3 victory at Grimsby on the last day of the season ensured that it got no worse, but Doncaster still had to face the indignity of having to seek re-election.

'I knew that we had to make a lot of changes during the summer. We were desperate to get some scoring power and also some attitude into the club. I got a couple of players from Celtic, John Dowie and Billy Russell. I went back to Hull City for Alan Warboys, and I signed Hugh Dowd and Ian Nimmo from Sheffield Wednesday. My best signing, though, was probably Les Cocker, who used to put me through my paces at Elland Road. He joined me as assistant manager and I was very glad to have him on board. He had been one of the driving forces of our physical welfare at Elland Road until he had left to assist Don Revie with the England job. When Don threw in the England manager's job, Les was left at a loose end and I was delighted when he joined me at Doncaster.'

Although there was a tremendous job to be done to pull Doncaster Rovers round, and perhaps even take the club up and out of Division Four which had been its paddock since 1971, Billy was totally committed. While everyone else took in the summer sun he devoted all his time to plotting the future of the club. When the new season dawned there appeared to be an immediate improvement. The League Cup started the new campaign and Rovers were to play local rivals Sheffield United in the opening round. The Blades were then in the Third Division, but still a major force, and a 1–1 draw at Bramall Lane was a very good result. Even better was the 3–1 success at home in the return leg – and even more encouraging was the 8,444 crowd that turned up to see it.

By the time the League programme got under way, optimism was high in the Doncaster camp. However, some very good results were marred by some equally bad ones. But the worst event of all took place on 4 October 1979 as a training session came to an end.

'Les Cocker had said that he wasn't feeling well but that he was sure he could work it off,' Billy recalled. 'We were finished for the day when Les suddenly collapsed and died. We were all shocked, and I was especially stunned. He was only fifty-five and I had known him and worked with him for a good many of those years. He was a terrific guy, marvellous with players,

131

dedicated to his job and the game, altogether a very nice man.'

Possibly as a token of how they felt, Doncaster Rovers won each of their next six matches, dedicating every success to Les Cocker. A defeat at Northampton was a rare blot on the record sheet as Doncaster entered December with just that one loss in a run of thirteen games. The magic touch of Billy Bremner was not only working on the pitch. The turnstiles were clicking much faster and more often too. In the previous two seasons, visits by Aldershot had been watched by fewer than 1,600 people on each occasion. In the 1979/80 season, the same fixture attracted 6,210.

The Christmas season was a little unkind. Darlington, Walsall and Huddersfield inflicted successive defeats on Rovers and Bremner was far from happy about it – especially when he had an argument with a referee and was subsequently charged with 'bringing the game into disrepute'. He was fined £200 and warned about his conduct in the future.

'It's a joke when that sort of thing happens,' said Bremner. 'You get some referees who are so officious it's just not true. They consider themselves to be above question. Players and managers often have their entire careers and livelihoods resting on one result, and yet they are expected to be so disinterested that they will turn a blind eye to blatantly wrong decisions without saying a word about them. If any of my players were so lacking in passion that they didn't care if the referee made a mistake, I would want to know what they thought they were doing by trying to earn a living as a professional footballer. I know that there is a limit, and I know that there are right ways and wrong ways of airing your views, but football is about people – not robots.'

That was his view at the time, and it continued to be his view over the years. He hated the injustice of bad refereeing decisions and would often sound off about such things, even when he had been watching a televised game from the neutrality of his armchair.

As the Christmas period passed, all the good work of the first half of the season was undone by a string of bad results. A

5–0 home win over local rivals Scunthorpe in mid-February was the single silver lining in an otherwise dense black cloud of seventeen games with just that one victory. Had the Bremner magic worn off? Billy had no such thoughts.

'We went through a sort of confidence crisis, and that seriously affected our results, but I think the chief problem was that we could not train properly in the bad weather. We had no facilities when I joined the club and matters finally came to a head that winter. One day I found myself taking the players to a local leisure centre, otherwise we simply would have been unable to train. The players had to queue with other users of the place while I paid for them one by one to go through the turnstiles. You can imagine what that sort of thing did for team morale. It is absolutely vital that footballers feel good about themselves. When they are forced to face the realization that they are playing for a club that has such serious limitations, it affects their self-confidence in a bad way. After the leisure centre episode, however, we did manage to make arrangements with RAF Finningley to use their facilities, and we began negotiations to use a privately owned aircraft hangar adjoining the ground. We definitely had to make some progress if we were going to move forward!'

As the weather improved, so did the results, and Doncaster finished the season in mid-table. Possibly the game that delighted Billy the most was a 1–0 win at home to Bournemouth in March 1980. Doncaster had an injury crisis at the time and Billy gave himself the No. 10 shirt. That victory came after a run of three successive defeats and there were many who said that he should have played more often. The following season he did – and what a season it was.

That 1980/81 season was probably the nearest thing to a white-knuckle ride you could get at a football club. A run of victories would be followed by a heavy defeat and a run of defeats by convincing victory. There were such contrasts as a 5–0 defeat at Darlington and a 5–1 victory over Hereford. But, with only twelve defeats in forty-six Division Four matches, Doncaster Rovers achieved promotion.

What a celebration there was as Rovers achieved what few had thought would ever be possible again. The club's financial situation was far from good, even though the attendances had improved so dramatically. Bremner had been unable to buy success through expensive players and had been forced to work with a small squad, many of whom were only teenagers – among them Ian Snodin who later played for Leeds, Everton and Oldham.

'Doncaster Rovers was a great education for me,' said Snodin. 'Especially with Billy Bremner as my boss. You knew, when he told you something, that you were getting the benefit of his vast experience. He was great with the young players. He had obviously not forgotten what it was like to be starting out on your career. He could be hard at times, but you always knew that it was for your own good, and his success proved his point.'

With four clubs being promoted, Doncaster ensured its place among them in the penultimate game of the season – at home to Bournemouth. The Belle Vue ground had not seen as many as the 11,373 that crowded in since a League Cup tie with Derby nearly five years before. There was a wonderful party atmosphere as promotion was finally clinched.

'It was lovely to see,' Billy recalled. 'I like to see smaller clubs doing well because it provides such grand memories for their supporters. With big clubs, success is already expected and every few years there is something or other to celebrate – even if it is only getting to a Cup semi-final. With clubs like Donny, there is a hard core of supporters who are the greatest optimists in the world. They are high on hope, but low on expectation, and they never give up on their chosen club. When they do have something to celebrate it is a major highlight, a moment that they will remember for ever.'

The very last match of the season ended in a draw at Mansfield and took Rovers to a final third place, their best position for ten years. The club was in need of attendances around the 10,000 mark to break even but Rome, as they say, was not built in a day and, since there had been a substantial

Leading Leeds to triumph against Real Saragossa in 1966. (POPPERFOTO)

Back at Elland Road – this time as manager! (COLORSPORT)

Billy scores against Ujpest Dozsa in the European Cup in 1974. (COLORSPORT)

Bremner in civvies, on his way to the 1975 European Cup final. (POPPERFOTO)

Bremner and Johann Cruyff exchange pleasantries before the 1975 European Cup final. (POPPERFOTO)

Juventus are beaten and Leeds take home the 1971 Fairs Cup. (POPPERFOTO)

Billy scores against Barcelona on the way to the 1975 European Cup final. (COLORSPORT)

Scotland has qualified for the 1974 World Cup. Another of Bill's proudest moments (above). (COLORSPORT)

Here he is in action against Wales in 1974 (left) and posing for the camera (right) before playing against Northern Ireland in the same year. (COLORSPORT)

Scotland draw with Yugoslavia in the 1974 World Cup, going out heartbreakingly on goal difference. (COLORSPORT)

Billy takes a fancy to Martin Chivers's shirt in the 1972 Scotland – England clash. (COLORSPORT)

Glad to be here – Bremner at the 1974 World Cup tournament. (POPPERFOTO)

Billy Bremner surges forward for Scotland. (COLORSPORT)

Minutes away from the final whistle as Scotland beat Zaire 2–0 in the 1974 World Cup. (COLORSPORT)

Inches away from making history. Bremner's efforts scrape the post as Scotland draw 0–0 with Brazil in the 1974 World Cup. (COLORSPORT)

increase, the future did at least look promising. Billy Bremner himself, however, was not blinded by optimism.

'I knew that I would have to be making do financially. There was no money at all to be spending on players. We were trying to develop the club's youth policy so that, in the long term, the prospects of a healthier bank balance would be much better. Cyril Knowles had been the youth-team coach, but he had a good offer to go to Middlesbrough. When we lost Cyril, we replaced him with David Pugh. Other than that small change – and the signing of Colin Douglas from Celtic – we remained much the same into the next season. I wanted to give everyone a chance to show what they could do in the Third Division and also to help the club consolidate a little with the extra revenue gained from increased sponsorships.'

A home defeat by Reading opened the curtain on the 1981/82 League season, but the following six games soon dispelled any potential gloom. A draw at Bristol City was followed by five successive victories.

There was a distraction when Doncaster were drawn to play Crystal Palace in the League Cup after knocking out Chesterfield in the first round. Rovers won the first leg, but lost the second and were eliminated, although they had put up a creditable performance. In November of that season, Rovers hit a very bad patch in which they gained just three points from eleven games.

'We had terrible injury problems. I signed Terry Cooper and he did his best but, in truth, we only had a small squad and we were really stretched. I even played myself a couple of times, just as I had in the previous season. I had hung up my boots before I joined Doncaster, but in an emergency I had to make myself available, didn't I? It was good to play again but it would have been even better under different circumstances.'

Doncaster slid down the table at a rather alarming rate but, just like a bungee jumper reaching the end of his line, they bounced back up again by losing just three games in the last nineteen. Rovers finished the season in nineteenth place and preserved their status in Division Three for another year. Terry

Cooper left at the end of the season to further his own managerial career, and there were also several other changes – most of them sideways moves rather than improvements.

'It was a real experience as manager of Doncaster. In many ways it was probably a better education than if I had waited and taken an appointment with a much bigger club. I really enjoyed myself at Donny. I did have my disagreements, of course, but none of them are worth recalling. It was an honest little club and I wanted to do my best for it, even if there were some serious limitations.'

The 1982/83 season was a pretty dismal one. Only nine matches were won out of the forty-six played in the Third Division, and there were not too many happy memories as Rovers slipped back into Division Four once again. However, there had been an amazing sequence of games in September 1982, the like of which even Billy Bremner had never before experienced.

'It started with a 6–1 win over Exeter City. Our next home game was against Reading and I think we all had to keep pinching ourselves to make sure that we were not dreaming. Why? Well, the final result was 7–5 in our favour, but I had never seen a game like it, before or since, as the advantage kept swinging back and forth. Our next home game was very similar, except that this time we lost 6–3 to Wigan and then, in our fourth consecutive home match we drew 4–4 with Brentford. It was a memorable few weeks because the Belle Vue fans had seen thirty-six goals in four matches. I wish that the rest of the season had been as memorable, but it wasn't. We lost twenty-six of our League matches – and that, of course, could only mean one thing.'

Doncaster did not finish at the bottom of the Third Division – that dubious honour fell to Chesterfield – but Rovers were only one place better off and went down with them. In just over four years, Billy Bremner had changed the fortunes of Doncaster Rovers, but now he had to start all over again. It might have been easier to resign, but Bremner had never been a quitter.

In many ways it might have seemed like the end of the world when Doncaster Rovers were demoted again, but the gloom soon lifted – especially when the new season started with a very convincing 3–0 win over Wrexham at home. The downside of it was that there were only 2,189 in attendance at Belle Vue to see it. That turned out to be the smallest home crowd of the season, though, because the 'wait-and-see' brigade who had stayed at home on the opening day were soon encouraged to give Doncaster some support. To prove that the emphatic victory over Wrexham had been no fluke, Billy Bremner's boys then won 2–1 at Mansfield and drew 1–1 at Scunthorpe in the League Cup – the return leg bringing a decisive 3–0 victory.

Of course, there had to be the inevitable sobering effect of defeat and there were, in fact, three in the early part of the season. They are worth mentioning because they turned out to be rarities in a season which ended up being a very good one indeed. Reading, Hartlepool and Torquay had all conquered Doncaster in Division Four matches by the end of October, but it was then two months before another defeat. Doncaster slipped to seventh place after that defeat by Torquay but that was to be their lowest placing all season.

'We gradually gained confidence and we only lost five more League games all that season,' said Bremner. 'It was really good to see the players enjoying themselves again and the supporters having something to shout about. We were also helped when the board was joined by Peter Wetzel, who made some cash available to strengthen the squad. I bought John Philliben from Stirling Albion for £60,000, which was a club record at the time. He was a very good young defender. I also bought Jim Dobbin from Celtic for £25,000 and Alan Brown from Shrewsbury for £35,000, and so I had been able to strengthen the squad in the defence, the midfield and the attack.'

Attendances steadily increased until Belle Vue was taking in virtually twice as many fans at the end of the season as it had seen at the start. The club was still losing money, though, and by the end of the season the overall debt had grown to £170,000. That was the perpetual black cloud, but there was a beautiful silver lining of promotion. Several weeks before that was finally clinched, however, Doncaster had an amazing experience playing away to Northampton.

'Our coach broke down about fifty miles from Northampton,' Billy Bremner recalled. 'We were really stuck until we started to see supporters on their way to the game. To save time, the players changed into their kit in the coach while we flagged down supporters to see what room they had in their cars. We managed to get everyone to the ground in a fleet of private cars, but it was touch and go. The match was actually held up for eleven minutes but everyone understood the problem and knew that we had done our best not to cause a delay. The best was yet to come, though, because we beat Northampton 4–1. It made me think that perhaps we ought to thumb our way to matches more often.'

York City were champions of Division Four with a massive 101 points, but Doncaster's tally of 85 was enough to give them second place. Once again there were celebrations in South Yorkshire.

Bremner made few changes to his playing staff. He paid £30,000 to bring John Buckley to the club from Partick Thistle and he signed Aidan Butterworth from Leeds. Apart from those two, there were no changes to the squad.

'Things had improved but there was still not the sort of money to go out and just buy what I wanted. That is something that is often forgotten by supporters. Managers are either given a budget or have to seek board approval for each individual signing. There is not always the cash available to do exactly what you want and then, if there is money to hand, you can't always spend it because you can't find what you are looking for. Spending just for the sake of it is not only stupid, it's suicidal, because you can break your bank and find that there is nothing in the kitty when you have an emergency.'

The new season back in Division Three started with an almost predictable defeat, just as the others had. A visit to

Preston ended in a 2–0 loss but, once that was out of the way, Doncaster went on to better things – namely five wins in six games. A 4–1 success at Reading was particularly good. By the end of November, Rovers were looking like possible promotion candidates once again.

'It was the old story. While we had a settled side we were doing well but, when the New Year came in and we started getting a few injuries and became involved in a bit of a run in the FA Cup, things started to fall apart a little. We reached the fourth round of the FA Cup after we beat Rochdale and Altrincham in the first two rounds and then Queen's Park Rangers in the third. When we played QPR, they were fourteenth in the First Division and had just beaten West Ham 3–1 away from home. When we beat them 1–0 it was a bit of a giant killing for Donny. We went out in the next round at Everton who beat us 2–0, but we gave them a few scares and there were nearly 40,000 fans applauding us off the park at the end of the game. It was a great experience for the Doncaster players.'

Doncaster finished in fourteenth place, gaining a few memorable results along the way, but most importantly they would still be in Division Three the following season. Elsewhere there were catastrophes at the end of the season as firstly the game was struck by horror at the Bradford City fire and then, soon afterwards, the violent tragedy of the Heysel Stadium.

'I saw the events on television,' said Billy, 'and I could not believe my own eyes. I had seen a few things before that I would rather forget but that has to be the blackest month that football has ever known. It almost seems innocuous to mention that Donny was affected because of the improvements that had to be made at the stadium. It was touch and go as to whether the safety regulations would be met before the start of the new season, with people working round the clock in order to satisfy the authorities. We were given permission to play our first game but it was a close call.'

During the summer there was transfer activity, some of it to help raise some cash for the necessary ground alterations. Ian Snodin was sold to Leeds for £200,000, while his brother Glynn went to Sheffield Wednesday for £115,000. There were a few other changes with about £60,000 being spent on new players. Ray Deans had been signed from Clyde for £40,000 during the latter part of the 1984/85 season, so Doncaster had a new look for the start of their 1985/86 campaign.

With an opening run of seven games without defeat, Doncaster were off to a flying start. They then lost a couple of matches but bounced back immediately to win a couple, including an excellent 2–1 win at Wolves. In October 1985 there were developments elsewhere which would create more than just ripples at Doncaster. Leeds were struggling in the Second Division and manager Eddie Gray was dismissed. It was not long before the obvious became a reality and Billy Bremner was appointed manager of the club, following in the footsteps of his mentor, Don Revie.

'I had grown to love Donny. When I wanted to get into management I had no intention of going straight to a big club. I wanted to learn the trade and Doncaster had given me a great opportunity to do that. It was with a heavy heart that I left there, but I could not turn down such an exciting challenge as becoming manager of Leeds United – I just couldn't.'

13

BACK AT ELLAND ROAD

Leeds United were languishing in the middle of the Second Division when Billy Bremner returned to Elland Road as the new manager in October 1985. At one point they had been as low as twentieth after a 6–2 defeat at Stoke. Eddie Gray had been in charge and the only reservation that Bremner had about following him into the management hot seat was that the fans might have thought that he was cashing in on Gray's misfortune.

'Eddie and I were pals and I was really sorry for him when he went. I knew he would not suffer too much because he was a typical Scot, a survivor. However, I would have willingly stayed as manager of Doncaster Rovers if it had meant him keeping his job at Leeds. He had been battling against the odds for some time. The club was in a mess and trying to manage a club in those circumstances was like trying to sweep up dead leaves in a gale.'

Bremner sought short-term answers to the problems. Denis Irwin and Andy Linighan were both sold to Oldham, Terry Phelan was given a free transfer and joined Wimbledon, and Scott Sellars eventually went to Blackburn after requesting a transfer. They were young players and were probably good for the future, but Billy Bremner was concerned only with the present.

The first months in charge were difficult, to say the least. Victories were scarce. Games against South London clubs seemed to be particularly unwelcome as a trip to Millwall resulted in a 3–1 defeat, and a week later a home match against Crystal Palace also ended in a 3–1 loss. A few weeks later a visit to Charlton resulted in a 4–0 defeat. When Wimbledon were beaten 3–0 away it came as quite a surprise. The relegation zone was beckoning and Billy's hair seemed to be going grey at a rate of knots.

It was not until Huddersfield were beaten 2–0 at home at the start of March that some sort of self-belief began to seep into the side. A few bad results followed and Leeds slumped to eighteenth place, but there was a new wave of optimism at the club and the scorelines began to take on a much healthier look. Consecutive away victories at Portsmouth and Bradford City followed by a 3–1 avenging of Millwall at Elland Road saw Leeds move to the middle of the table, and that was where they stayed, finishing in fourteenth place.

'Being manager of the club was totally different from before. Leeds was still a very big club with tremendous support, but there was a lot of work to be done,' said Billy. 'It was great to be back at Elland Road where everything was so familiar to me. At times I almost expected Don Revie to walk in and tell me to get out of his chair. Yet, somehow, the place seemed run down and I knew that the only way to build it up again was to get the right results on the park as quickly as possible. It was not enough to say that we were safe from relegation. We had to be battling for promotion and I spent most of the summer working on the changes that would, hopefully, achieve that. I enjoyed the training and coaching with the players, but there is always a lot more to a manager's job than that. I never wondered if I was up to it, but there were times when I wondered if it could not have been just a little easier. I think my biggest problem was that I felt I had to be personally involved in everything, whether it was coaching or going to look at players. It was quite exhausting and made me appreciate all the more what it had taken for Don Revie to have been so successful.'

Bremner took his own coaching and management team to Leeds when he moved from Doncaster Rovers, and together they set about turning their squad into a unit that would follow proudly in the footsteps of the squads in which Bremner himself had played. They came down to earth with a bump on the opening day of the 1986/87 season when Blackburn beat them 2–1 at Ewood Park. Stoke were then beaten 2–1 at home a few days later but, when Sheffield United visited Elland Road a few days after that and walked away with a 1–0 victory, confidence began to drain away again.

Billy Bremner talked to his players, coaxed them, shouted at them, and told them exactly what they were representing when they pulled on a Leeds United shirt. It seemed to do the trick too because there followed only one defeat in the next ten League games. Suddenly Leeds were promotion candidates and the crowds began to grow at Elland Road. Some mixed results followed, which saw a slight dip in the League position and a low ebb was reached again in the last game before Christmas – a visit to Stoke City, which the year before had resulted in a 6–2 defeat. It could not be that bad again, could it?

'It was one of those horror games,' remembered Billy. 'We were 5–0 down at half-time. I couldn't believe what I was watching. Everything that we had instilled in the previous months seemed to be forgotten, and Stoke had themselves an early Christmas party. At half-time, I had a few things to say and, as a result, the second half was not so bad. If you like, we drew 2–2 in the second half. I prefer to think of that rather than remember it as a 7–2 beating. When you get into goal difference at the end of a season, results like that can kill you off completely.'

There was a recovery, however. It did not come as quickly as Bremner might have liked but, as the season wore on, his side gathered strength and, after dipping down to eighth place, they worked hard to get back to fourth. That was good enough to take part in the new play-off system – the teams finishing from third to fifth in the Second Division and the team finishing third from bottom in the First Division would engage in a knockout competition to decide who would be in the top division along with the two top clubs from the Second Division for the following season.

'I didn't like the idea at first. It seemed wide open to injustice to me,' said Bremner. 'I thought that it would be very unfair for a club that had worked hard all season and finished third to find themselves having a bad game in the play-offs and losing out to a team that might have had fewer points than themselves.'

Leeds suffered just four League defeats after Christmas and steadily climbed the table to clinch their play-off place – but they were also forging ahead on a different front, the FA Cup. They had to work hard to beat non-League Telford in the third round, but looked much more comfortable in the following round when they beat Swindon 2–1 away. Queen's Park Rangers went next and, after Wigan were disposed of in the quarter-finals, Leeds were just one game away from a trip to Wembley for the first time since Bremner himself had been skipper of the side.

There was a small matter of trying to beat Coventry to get to the FA Cup Final, and the two teams met at Hillsborough in mid-April. What followed was one of the most thrilling semi-finals for years. The match was televised live after a delay to the kick-off because of the number of fans still trying to get into the ground at noon, when the match had been due to start.

Bremner had fired his men up for the game as if their very lives depended upon it and they stormed into Coventry from the moment that the whistle blew. The Midlanders were rocked back on their heels and, as early as the fourteenth minute, they fell behind when Micky Adams took a perfect corner and David Rennie headed it home. To say that Coventry were under the cosh would be an understatement. But for the brilliance of Steve Ogrizovic in their goal, the game would probably have been wrapped up by half-time.

During the break, Bremner ordered more of the same and it certainly seemed that the ineffective Coventry attack would never be able to break down the tight defence of Leeds – that is, not until there were little more than twenty minutes to go. A mistake by the Leeds captain, Brendan Ormsby, gave Dave Bennett the chance to put the ball across the Leeds goal, and

Micky Gynn thumped home the equalizer. It then became Leeds' turn to come under pressure as Coventry went for glory. Keith Houchen gave them a 2–1 lead and all looked lost until Andy Ritchie sent a cross sailing over for Keith Edwards to head into the net. The last five minutes or so were played at fever pitch but the score remained at 2–2. Extra-time was played at the same pace, but Dave Bennett grabbed the winner for Coventry and, despite enormous Leeds pressure, they held on to take the match 3–2 and make their first Wembley appearance, which ended in an historic victory over Tottenham.

'I could not be upset with my players, they were magnificent,' said Bremner. 'They ran their tails off, tackled like terriers and at the end they were totally exhausted. They had given all that they could give and nobody could ask for more than that. I was very proud of them and I was also proud of the supporters who had been tremendous from start to finish. Of course, I would have loved to have won the match, but I took a lot of encouragement from the way that the team had played. It told me that they were capable of even greater things.'

That was not the only dramatic game of the season. The play-offs were still to come. Oldham had finished above Leeds, and those two clubs met in one semi-final, while Charlton from the top division had to meet Ipswich. At Elland Road, Leeds won 1–0 thanks to a Keith Edwards goal, and it was Edwards who provided an even more important strike when the two teams met again at Boundary Park in the second leg. Oldham won that game 2–1 but, because of Edwards' away goal, Leeds went through.

Leeds met Charlton in the final. There was no Wembley appearance in those days, the two teams doing battle over home and away legs. The first leg was at Charlton, the Londoners winning 1–0. Two days later, they met again at Elland Road and Brendan Ormsby gave a real captain's performance, scoring the only goal of the match. A third meeting became necessary, at Birmingham City's ground, St Andrews. It seemed that nothing was going to separate the two teams and, with the score at 0–0, extra-time became unavoidable. It was Leeds who finally broke the deadlock when John Sheridan put the ball in the net. It stayed like that until seven minutes from the end when, amid much clock watching, Charlton equalized through Peter Shirtliff, who then broke the hearts of the Leeds fans by hitting a winner moments before the final whistle.

'I could not believe that we had lost out after all that,' said Billy. 'I don't think that Charlton were in the game for most of the time. Their goals were well taken and the difference between the two sides was simply that they scored and we didn't, but it was cruel on my players and the Leeds fans who had travelled to Birmingham. Heads went down and there were tears, almost as if we had been relegated. I had to remind them all that, while we had not won promotion, we had turned a major corner in the fortunes of the club and there were better days ahead. It took me back to the early days at Leeds when we were branded as the team who always went close but never actually won anything. We shut the critics up then and I knew we could do it again.'

By the time the next season was ready to roll, Leeds United had been made favourites for promotion. All Billy Bremner's side had to do was fulfil the promise they had shown.

The 1987/88 season began with promise. The first five games produced two victories and three draws but, by mid-October, it was clear that there was a scoring problem. After eleven Second Division matches, only five goals had been scored and, from a promising fourth position, Leeds slipped to twelfth after a 1–1 draw at Blackburn at the start of October. A 3–1 home defeat by Aston Villa was followed by a 6–3 loss at Plymouth. Leeds were now in the lower half of the division.

'We had a few injuries, but you cannot always blame every problem on injuries. We seemed to have lost confidence in front of goal,' said Bremner. 'It wasn't that the team were playing particularly badly, but we just seemed to have a big problem with getting the ball into the net. That put extra pressure on our defence and we began to ship goals. In fairness, it was a rare thing to be able to select our strongest side. Mark

Aizlewood had a lengthy lay-off, as did David Rennie, John Sheridan, John Pearson and Bob Taylor. It was not until they were all available together that we started getting some decent results again.'

There was a revival in December when Leeds won six consecutive games and, despite a few setbacks, managed to keep up that form to finish just outside the play-off places. A 5–0 home win over local rivals Sheffield United was probably the highlight of the season, except for one special day in early November when Leeds beat Shrewsbury 2–1 at Elland Road. It was special because it was the day that David Batty made his debut.

'David had been doing really well in the reserves and in training, and I could not help but give him a try. I saw a lot of myself in him. He was not the biggest of guys but he was absolutely fearless. He tackled like a real Yorkshire terrier. He was still very young when I gave him his first-team chance during an injury crisis, but I had worked with him a lot and I was sure he could perform. At the end of the game we had won and he had done all that was asked of him. I did not keep him in the first team after that because I needed more experienced players to steer us out of a bad patch, but I knew I could select him at any time and he would not let me down.'

David Batty recalled his progress at Leeds and the encouragement he received from his boss.

'Everyone at Leeds looked up to Billy. It's very easy to start calling a person a legend, but he really lived up to it. Even then, in training, he was terrific and made you feel that he could take your job any time he liked and prove that he could do it better. He used to talk to me about my career and my ambitions, and he used to give me lots of tips on playing. He was like a father figure to me and many of the other young players at Leeds. He never treated you like anything less than a professional footballer and he was constantly seeking ways of giving you confidence and self-belief.

'He was always willing to listen to your problems and to help out with them if it was possible. I kept in touch with Billy long after we had both left Leeds. He was a good friend, willing to advise and listen to your ups and downs. I could not have wished for a better start to my career than being under the wing of Billy Bremner.'

John Sheridan became something of a penalty king that season. He scored seven of them, plus five other goals, making him the top League scorer for Leeds. A final flurry of two wins and two draws in the last four games helped the club to finish in seventh place. Among those last games was a 1–0 win over Crystal Palace, which put paid to that club's hopes of making the play-offs.

'We finished in a respectable position but on the whole the season had been disappointing,' said Bremner. 'We had gone out of the FA Cup after one game and we had done little better in the League Cup. It was one of those seasons that was full of ifs and buts, and one which I was glad to forget.'

Bremner had had his contract extended before the start of the 1987/88 season, but there had been talk that he might not stay if his ambitions for the club were not realized sooner rather than later. However, he was still there at the start of the 1988/89 season – for a while at least.

The new season began terribly. A 1–1 draw at home to Oxford might not have been so bad had it not been followed by a 4–0 mauling at Portsmouth a few days later. Drawn games against Manchester City and Bournemouth followed, and even a 2–0 win over Barnsley at Elland Road failed to lift the gloom that was descending upon Leeds United. A 2–0 defeat at home by Chelsea put Leeds into eighteenth place. Something had to give. The board were getting a lot of stick from the supporters and, of course, board members are famed throughout the land for ignoring the accusing fingers and assuming that they are pointing at someone else. In this case they believed they were meant for Billy Bremner. The day after he had steered Leeds to a 2–1 win over Peterborough in the first leg of a League Cup tie, he was called into the office and told that his services would no longer be required. He was given a pay-off and the press was informed. The jungle drums had already been beating in Leeds, though, and a large contingent of fans had gathered at Elland Road to find out what was happening.

'I came out of the building to get into my car and, as well as the media men, there was a big crowd of fans. I didn't know what to expect. I could understand them being angry about the lack of success, they felt exactly as I did myself. They closed in on me and then held out their hands for me to shake. They were marvellous and they gave me a real lift. I could take the sack but I didn't want to lose the affection of the fans. I thought the world of them and I hope that they felt the same way about me.'

They did, Billy!

Billy Bremner returned to his home and, not for the first time, settled down to contemplate his future. He could not come to terms with the idea that his football career had come to an end and he began to keep an eye on the goings-on at the smaller clubs again. Nothing happened until the following summer of 1989. The Hillsborough disaster had saddened him as it had everyone else, and he wondered again if he should forget about being directly involved in football and concentrate on the media work which had proved to be both enjoyable and reasonably rewarding.

In June 1989 Doncaster Rovers, still his local side, had a change of ownership. Joe Kinnear was the manager at the club, which had just been relegated back into the Fourth Division. He had gone on holiday with the promise that his job was safe, a promise given by chairman Bernie Boldry. However, by the time he came back, Doncaster Rovers had been taken over by a new consortium, he had been dismissed and Billy Bremner had been installed as the new manager.

'I think they had to move quickly,' said Bremner. 'The local council had issued a High Court writ for money owed, and I don't think there were enough funds available for the club to respond favourably. They had just been through a terrible season and they were still in debt, even though they had raised nearly a quarter of a million pounds in transfers. They needed to get more people through the turnstiles and interested enough to spend more in sponsorships and commercial sales. All of that, however, depended heavily upon success on the pitch and that just wasn't happening.

'Mike Collett was the new chairman, and he told me that he wanted a five-year plan to get Doncaster Rovers into the Second Division, and that he would be able to raise some cash with a new share issue. It sounded good to me and so I decided to give it a go. There were only about seventeen professional players when I joined the club and I wanted a fresh start, so I changed a few of the faces and started work on organizing the side to get the best out of the talent available.'

The five-year plan began a little hesitantly. A single-goal defeat at Exeter on the opening day did not augur well, and the next few games did not make things any better. A goalless home draw with Gillingham was followed by a 2–1 defeat at Lincoln and then a 3–0 loss at home to Peterborough. As the League tables began to take on some sort of shape, Billy's men found themselves just two places away from the lowest possible place in the entire League structure.

'I could not stand to look at the Division Four table. I kept wanting to turn it upside down. We just had not got it together at that time.'

A 2–1 victory away to Scarborough was more promising but, just as the smiles were beginning to break out at Belle Vue, the club suffered two more defeats – both at home – to Southend and Aldershot. On both occasions the scoreline was 1–0. Bremner read the riot act – these performances were simply not good enough. The players responded with a 6–0 win away to Hartlepool. At last it seemed that something was beginning to happen. Once again, though, there was disappointment as the club suffered five defeats and two draws before securing their next victory.

That was the pattern for the rest of the season, with Doncaster Rovers staying near the bottom of the Fourth Division. The last two games really typified the rest of the season as Doncaster beat Rochdale 4–0 and then lost 4–1 at

Scunthorpe. Doncaster finished the season in twentieth place.

The nation was still recovering from watching the 1990 World Cup when Bremner began another season in charge of Doncaster Rovers. The new campaign was barely a few days old when Rotherham visited for a League Cup tie first leg. The match held plenty of drama and, at half-time, Rotherham were just ahead with a 3–2 scoreline. In the second half they ran riot, however, and finally went home with a 6–2 victory. The home fans could have been forgiven for thinking, 'Here we go again,' but Doncaster's League form was a totally different proposition. The opening game was a 3–2 success at Carlisle, and that was followed by a run of victories over Wrexham, Halifax, Rochdale and Walsall. Doncaster were top of the table with maximum points after the first five games and had equalled the club record for the best start to a season.

They were unable to improve on that record as four successive defeats followed and Doncaster were on that white-knuckle ride once again. From the beginning of November, Rovers went nine games without defeat and shot back to the top of the Fourth Division. Attendances were improving again, too, and the prospects were looking good but, as in the past, it wasn't to last. Not only were there players missing because of their injuries, but others, from what was a very small squad, were having to play out of position to compensate for them. Doncaster failed to win any of their last eight games as a season that had begun so well disintegrated completely. The club finished in eleventh place, a great improvement on the previous season but a disappointment nevertheless.

When Bremner joined the club, Steve Beaglehole had moved in with him as assistant manager. Dave Blakely had also moved from Leeds to take over the role of general manager. They had proved to be a winning team in the past and they were determined to be winners again. When the 1991/92 season dawned, they were as optimistic as ever.

'When we reflected on the previous season,' said Bremner, 'we could see that, although we were disappointed not to secure at least a play-off place, we had nevertheless made a lot of progress. It is never easy to change the fortunes of a small club with a debt constantly hanging round its neck, but we still felt that if we kept on plugging away we would get back to the Third Division, and possibly go even further.'

For a change the new season began with a home match. It might have been better if it had been away, because the Belle Vue fans were treated to seeing their side go down 3–0 to Carlisle. A week later Doncaster lost 3–2 at Scunthorpe. A week after that they lost 4–1 at home to Burnley – and then they lost 3–1 at Northampton. Four League matches played, four goals scored, thirteen conceded, and not a point in sight. To make matters worse, Doncaster had been knocked out of the League Cup during that same period by Crewe, by an aggregate of 9–4. Those six matches had seen twenty-two goals fly past the Doncaster defence.

There was the brief glimpse of a possible oasis when Wrexham were beaten 3–1 at the beginning of September – but it turned out to be just a mirage since the next three games were all lost. By the end of October, Doncaster had won just one game, drawn three, and lost nine League matches, putting them into twenty-third place in the table. Something had to be done.

Decisions were taken on 1 November 1991. Billy Bremner and Dave Blakely resigned their posts and Steve Beaglehole became caretaker manager.

'We were not getting anywhere. It was getting worse instead of better,' Billy Bremner recalled. 'It was obvious that my style had not worked this time. Dave Blakely's decision to leave was his own, as was Steve Beaglehole's to stay. My decision was also my own. I couldn't stand to see Donny getting into such a state. No matter what I tried, it was just not working and so, for the good of the club and for the players and the supporters, I thought that there should be a change now rather than later to give whoever was taking over the time to improve things. There were no hard feelings either way. I was still a local man and I followed Doncaster enthusiastically. It was because I had a feeling for Donny that I left.'

Billy Bremner never managed another club. His years as a player and a manager were finally over. But that was not the end of the Billy Bremner story – not by any means.

14

BREMNER ON GAMESMANSHIP

Billy Bremner was often described as tough, uncompromising, hard, even dirty at times, but he was never accused of being a dishonest player.

Gamesmanship is as much a part of football as the skills of a midfielder, a striker or a goalkeeper. Fans of any team will tell you all about the skills and abilities of their particular favourite player. It seems to work out that the older the fan, with his greater memory of players past, the more that fan appears to know what he is talking about. Of course, that's perfectly true – up to a point. Yes, they know all about the teamwork that they see take place on the field. They know all about the skills that they see, or have seen in the past. However, not surprisingly, the thing most often missed by the adoring fan is one of the most concealed arts of the profession – gamesmanship.

Gamesmanship is something which is practised, and accepted, as part of the stock in trade by most teams these days. It is probably more widespread now than it has ever been, and Billy Bremner was only too aware of the fact.

'Two things account for the increase in gamesmanship that goes on, in my opinion – the sheer professionalism of top-class footballers, and the tremendously high rewards which can be gained. I have to say that those rewards will only come if you prove yourself to be at the top of the class, in an ever more fiercely competitive market. When you play, you are playing for points and trophies, you're playing for high stakes. The old-fashioned view that "the game's the thing" has now gone right out of the window.

'At Elland Road they used to talk about a forward who once played there. He was a past master at the art of diving into the penalty area when he had been fouled a yard or so outside it. They said that he gained quite a few spot-kicks for Leeds that way, and for the other clubs that he played for in his time. That penalty-area diving, once a rarity, now goes on throughout world football. It happens on some ground or other every week of every season.

'They have tried to crack down as much as possible on this gamesmanship, but how often have you seen it happen? There are a couple of minutes to go and the one team is winning by a single goal. If a player on that team gets a chance he'll boot the ball into touch – over the stand if possible. There is time-wasting at throw-ins, there's the trick of lying on the ground feigning injury when you are winning by a narrow margin and time is nearly up. A few seconds gained like this can be extremely precious and, let's face it, you can hardly blame players for bending the rules when there is so much at stake on the result of the game. It's a bit like the golfer making the final putt, knowing that if he pulls it off he has won thousands – but if he misses . . .

'I can tell you that some teams carry this art of gamesmanship a little bit too far, though. Yes, even in Britain. I know for a fact that there are some teams who get detailed instructions about what to do should they be penalized within striking distance of their own goal. You'll see an opponent about to take a free kick. You'll see the wall of defenders standing ten yards back – but you'll also see one of those defenders a little way in front of the wall, nearer by far to the ball than the regulations allow. By the time the referee has sorted that one out, a few valuable seconds have ticked away and the player taking the kick may have been put off and lost his concentration.

'That's not the end of it either. The next time that the same thing happens it is another player who stands ahead of the wall to waste a few more seconds. If it happens a third time it will be another player's turn. In this way no one player risks coming under the referee's eye too often and therefore ending up by getting booked.'

There was a time when it could be said that success in football was only achieved on the basis of 'the survival of the fittest'. Now, it seems that the old adage should be changed to 'the survival of the wiliest'! Many would say, and Billy Bremner was one of them, that the tricks of gamesmanship really came to the fore with the arrival of foreign players in this country and the increased activity of British clubs overseas.

'We had a reputation at Leeds for being "dirty players", and I must say that I resented that tag. We certainly weren't little angels, we never did pretend to be that, but when we came up against some of our continental opponents we certainly had our eyes opened. Foreign players seemed to take exception to a good old-fashioned shoulder charge but they had no qualms about a few other tricks – off the field as well as on it.

'There was the time we played Standard Liege in the Fairs Cup. We went to Belgium and we certainly seemed to receive every courtesy when we asked to go down to the ground for a kickabout on the morning of the match. The coach took us straight to the ground, through the gates and right up to the dressing room. All we had to do was step down, get changed and we were ready to play. Mind you, the ground was like being back in Yorkshire. There was a pit-heap at one end and a blast furnace at the other, if you'd told us we were at Millmoor, Rotherham, we would probably have believed you.

'All that seemed to change when we returned a few hours later for the actual game. By this time the crowds were milling about the stadium and the coach had to move through the mass of people very slowly. When we got to the gates through which we had driven earlier in the day, there was no entrance for us. The man on the gates was adamant, he would not let us drive into the ground. In the end there was no alternative but for the players to climb down from the coach and fight their way through all those milling fans to their dressing room. When we got there, some joker had got there before us.

'Inside the dressing room, the windows had all been sealed and the room felt like the inside of a blast furnace. Try as we might, we could not get those windows open, and so we changed, sweating cobs and muttering to ourselves, longing for the minutes to tick by so that we could get out on the pitch and breathe some fresh air again. We thought we had got the last laugh, though, when we walked off the pitch at the end with the score at 0–0. Wrong again. When we got to the baths we found that the water was stone cold.'

The gamesmanship didn't end there for Standard Liege. Anything that changes the routine for a team can be upsetting, and the Belgian side must have been quite aware of that when they visited Elland Road for the return leg. Many fans will remember what happened.

'Standard's colours are usually red and white, and that was the strip we expected to see when they came out of the tunnel for the second leg. Not a bit of it! They were wearing an all-white strip, exactly the same as ours. They hadn't informed anyone of this change and we tried to reason with them and get them to change into their usual colours. They refused point-blank and, in the end, it was us who had to go back up the tunnel and change the colour of our strip. I can't think what they hoped to gain by this performance, apart from unsettling our team just before the game.'

That was not the only occasion when Leeds United were treated to unsettling incidents in European matches. In Leipzig the incident was not at the beginning of the game, but at half-time.

'To get to the pitch from the dressing room, you had to take a lift down. We had no trouble getting down for the kick-off and, as we walked off at half-time, the lift was there waiting to take us back up. On the way up it suddenly stopped and, although the operator seemed to be juggling with his switches, we remained stuck in that lift for nearly the whole of the interval.

'Don Revie was doing his nut, I can tell you. He had gone up to the dressing room just before half-time, ready to give us a few pointers on tactics. When we didn't appear he went almost hairless. We finally made it to the dressing room just in time for a mouthful of tea before we had to get back in that blasted lift for the return journey. The boss never had time to give us any sort of briefing. The funny thing about it is that the lift never gave any trouble on the return journey – or at any time afterwards.'

The same sort of thing happened in Zagreb, in Yugoslavia. It was the first leg of the Fairs Cup Final, which Leeds eventually lost. Again the incident happened during half-time, as Billy Bremner explained.

'We were a goal down at half-time and Revie began to give us a pep talk as soon as we got to the dressing room. He had hardly started when there was a tremendous banging and shouting at the door, then a head popped in and began to jabber away in Yugoslavian. We got rid of him eventually and the boss began to speak again. Within a few seconds there was another bout of banging and shouting, and another head appeared round the door. Don Revie never did get to finish his half-time summary. The place was like a madhouse!'

Playing in Italy was also an eye-opener for Leeds United. The art of gamesmanship was demonstrated to a high degree on one particular occasion – and Leeds player Mike O'Grady was the fall guy. Bremner remembered the incident well.

'It was in Naples. We were well into the game when I suddenly realized that the huge crowd were really giving us the bird. I couldn't understand the reason. I looked round and there was Mike O'Grady, staggering along in a sort of daze with blood pouring down his face. On the ground near by was Omar Sivori who looked as though he was dead, except for the fact that he was laughing. When I asked Mike what had been going on, his answer was almost unprintable. The sum total was: "The so-and-so butted me in the face – and then he just lay down!"

'The referee ignored Sivori on the ground, who was surrounded by an army of medics giving him treatment for his so-called injury, and booked Mike O'Grady. Mike had been having a great game up until then, but that booking put him right off. The butt in the face hadn't helped much either. If ever a guy was conned, that guy was Mike O'Grady – especially when Sivori finally got up, laughed in Mike's face, and sauntered away up the field.

'We'd had trouble before that game began, too. We were told to get out onto the pitch in plenty of time, to warm up and practise shooting in and passing, to get the feel of the pitch and the crowd atmosphere. We had some trouble getting onto the pitch because the door leading onto it was locked. After some pantomime we finally got it open and everything seemed okay until we got on the pitch and I indicated to the guy there that we wanted some footballs. He professed not to understand – or maybe he didn't want to. With no football in sight we had to resort to exercising and jumping up and down while the crowd of yelling Italians jeered at us. Needless to say, when the Italian team came out, every one of their players had a football at his feet.'

Billy Bremner was always well known for his argumentative nature, especially when it came to bad refereeing decisions. Yet, whatever trouble Billy ever had with referees – or even with players and fans – he still believed that the British way of doing things was best. Many of his arguments came because of the reputation pushed on to Leeds United as a 'dirty' side. Bremner was always forthright in his defence of his team and their style of play, but he still upheld the rule of fair play.

'You wouldn't find a Leeds player pulling an opponent's hair, spitting in his face, putting a finger in his eye, or doing any of the quite common and, in my opinion, unsporting acts which we often encountered on our trips abroad. I often heard supporters say, "I can't believe that the referee didn't see such and such an incident," after one of our European games. Believe me, we couldn't understand it either. Sometimes I got the impression from certain referees that if a player pulled out a gun and shot an opponent, the game would be waved on – or the victim would be cautioned for time wasting.

'We often came in for some stick in the early days, until people began to realize that Leeds United were playing good football, even if we were hard. Maybe some referees were subconsciously influenced by our reputation as a so-called "dirty" team in those early days. Whatever, I still believe that the British system of football justice is the best in the world. Having seen at close quarters a lot of what went on in games abroad, I know deep down that the British referee is the most impartial anywhere. Yes, of course I've had my differences, but what player or manager hasn't?

'I believe that football is a man's game and, if you can't take a knock or two – and this applies to fans as well as players – then you shouldn't be having anything to do with the game. Referees are there to see that the game is played within the rules and in a fair way, but the excitement of the game can affect everyone and this has often led to misunderstandings. Gamesmanship, too, is not the prerogative of the foreign clubs. Let me tell you something about a cunning old fox called Joe Mercer.

'We were to play Manchester City – where Joe was the manager – in an FA Cup tie, in which victory would mean that we would be in the semi-finals again. We were really confident of pulling it off, especially after Joe Mercer had said his piece to the press. In every pre-match press statement that I saw, Mercer had indicated that he was coming to Elland Road with his team in the hopes of getting a draw, and then taking us to Maine Road for a replay.

'We had been warned about falling for the sucker punch because it had happened to us once before. When Zaragoza had come to Elland Road for a Fairs Cup play-off, we had been led to believe that they would be playing it tight at the back. Instead, they threw everything at us and, within fifteen minutes, they had slotted home three goals. We wouldn't fall for it again – or would we?

'We did. Joe Mercer's words were accepted at their face value . . . we fell for the sucker punch again. Right from the kick-off, City threw the lot at us. If they really had come intent on getting a draw, they must have thought that we were going to score a dozen! As it was, we were too busy trying to stem their onslaught to worry about scoring ourselves. We felt that this wasn't fair – they were supposed to be defending and here they were, like bats out of hell, going after goals. After all this time I have to admit that we must have been the luckiest team alive. We should have had a roasting, but Big Jack Charlton went up and scored us a goal and saved the day. How he managed it I shall never understand to this day. Inside the six-yard area were nine players – eight Manchester City men and Big Jack – and the ball went in the net.

'Well, Joe Mercer almost foxed us, but we lived to fight another day in the semi-final against Chelsea.'

Leeds United lost that semi-final. Then managed by Tommy Docherty, Chelsea had gone ahead with a goal by centre-forward Tony Hateley. It was dubbed the '£100,000 goal' by Docherty, who said of Hateley, 'That's what I bought him for.' With the score standing at 1–0, Leeds were awarded a free kick from just outside the Chelsea penalty area. Johnny Giles tapped the kick to Peter Lorimer who cracked home a vicious shot. The place erupted as the ball struck the back of the net and Leeds United had apparently equalized. But the goal was disallowed. Billy Bremner explained:

'When I say we were robbed, I mean we were robbed! We had been awarded the free kick but we had some trouble trying to get their players to line up, back ten yards from the ball. It was that gamesmanship all over again, trying to waste time. The referee was trying to sort it out as best he could. We were complaining that they were too near, they were reluctant to move, and everyone on both sides was tense and anxious.

'Eventually, the referee paced out his ten paces and turned around and gave a signal. We didn't hesitate, the ball was flicked to Peter Lorimer and he smashed it home into the Chelsea goal. Chelsea were absolutely stunned. All our players were in the air congratulating each other and the Leeds fans erupted in their delight. Then we realized that the referee was signalling for the kick to be taken again. There was no goal after all.

'Apparently, the Chelsea players had still not been standing the regulation distance from the ball and the signal, which we thought was for the kick to be taken, was for the Chelsea defenders to get back and line up where the referee was standing. They talk about that incident to this day in Leeds – and I still say, "We wuz robbed."'

Being put off your game, of course, is not always the intentional purpose of the opposition. Sometimes it is nothing to do with the opposition at all. Billy Bremner remembered a couple of occasions when Leeds United were put off for two very different reasons.

'The first occasion was when we were playing at Cardiff in a third-round FA Cup tie in 1964. As it happened, we won 1–0, which wiped out an ignominious hat-trick of three successive defeats by the Welsh club. All of them had been in the third round, all of them had been by a 2–1 margin, and all of them had been at Elland Road. Of course, all that happened before my time with the club.

'That, though, isn't the reason why I remember the game so vividly. No, it was the fact that this was the only game in which I played where not one, but two players broke a leg. McIntosh of Cardiff was first, then after another ten minutes it was the turn of Freddie Goodwin. It was just one of those things and there was nobody to blame for the two accidents, but the affair had everyone else on the field really worried. Everybody was scared stiff of going into a tackle in case it happened to them. It finished up with both sides playing as if they were in a practice game. It was a real case of "After you Claude . . . No, after you Cecil".

'The other time was when burned toast cost us a vital point. In my first season, 1959/60, when I made my League debut, we were eventually relegated to the Second Division, and I shall always remember how that one point would have allowed us to stay up.

'We had to get a point at Blackburn and then beat

Nottingham Forest at home. We had fixed up to have a meal in a hotel that we had never used before and on the menu was steamed chicken. There was also toast – and the toast had been badly burned. It was like a cinder and the very sight of it put us off and almost turned our stomachs. I know it sounds a bit stupid, but it's true, that meal put us all off our game and we lost by the odd goal in five.

'Don Revie played that day and he learned a good lesson. When he became manager and we had to go away for a match, or for the night before a game at Elland Road, everything had to be spot on for our peace of mind. Whenever we went abroad, the club doctor travelled with us and personally supervised our diets and accommodation.'

Gamesmanship knows few boundaries. A team famed for its superb passing will turn up for an away match to find that the grass has been only minimally cut in order to thwart their skills and technique. When the weather is particularly cold, the central heating in the visitors' dressing room can some-times mysteriously go wrong. Windows are left open for hours before the team arrives to ensure an 'icy reception'. More obvious are spoiling tactics on the pitch.

Bremner himself was sometimes used to tame certain members of the opposition when he played for Leeds. It didn't always work out the way that Billy intended, though, as he told me on one occasion.

'We were due to play Blackburn and they had this giant of a centre-half by the name of Mike England. He was just making a name for himself and I was the player who was detailed to go up in front of him and put him off his game. The idea was that I should keep on harassing him, even though he towered over me. I was nippy enough to get round him and I might even score a goal. It was a bit of a David and Goliath idea really, the only trouble was that this time it was Goliath who won.

'I buzzed around him, trying to niggle him into making a mistake. But, no matter how much I got stuck in, he never lost his composure once. He looked down at me with complete disdain and I could almost hear him thinking, "The midges are a bit troublesome this year!" '

Mike England, if he really did think that, must be the only player ever who regarded Billy Bremner as just 'troublesome'.

15

PELE AND THE OTHERS

Playing for so long with a big club like Leeds United, both in England and in Europe, meant that Billy Bremner came into contact with many star players. Names meant little to Bremner. He always considered himself, and his team-mates, to be as good as any member of the opposition. Don Revie cultivated that approach, especially when Leeds United were going out to face top-class opponents.

'You're the greatest,' Revie would tell them. 'So get out there, and don't worry about the things that they can do. Let them do the worrying about you.'

Revie's psychological approach certainly seemed to have worked as far as his club was concerned because Bremner and the rest of the team approached almost every game believing that they were more than a match for any opposition, whether it was British or European.

Of course, in many instances, a star player's reputation goes before him and the critics and the press are always eager to boost his abilities sky-high. Bremner, however, believed that no player was a superman, however fine a player he was.

'Some of those players were labelled as supermen by the press, but no amount of newsprint would have ever made them that. They were good players all right and, for the most part, they played good football. In this category I'd place men of my day, like Eusebio of Portugal, Helmut Haller of West Germany and Italy's Rivera.

'Eusebio rightly won a great reputation in the 1966 World Cup, with his ability to bend a free kick and score goals with a shot that seemed as if it came from a gun. He was a magnificent athlete, physically strong, and certainly menacing when he got into gear and was bearing down on the goal. The one thing that he didn't have was the understanding of when to hang on to the ball and when to part with it to advantage. I would place his team-mate of the time, Coluna, as a better all-rounder. Coluna, of course, dropped back from being an attacker to the middle line, but he never let a chance of attack go by if it came up. He was good in defence as well, though. Eusebio was all attack – he never went back to help in defence – and that, in my opinion, prevented him from being the complete footballer.'

Bremner was perhaps the most outspoken critic of foreign players who had been foisted on the British soccer-loving public as something extra special, and then proved to be little more than ordinary. But in the case of Pele, Billy was as full of praise as the next man.

'Pele was the one foreign player who I would rate as being able to stand up to the competition in a forty-two-match English First Division football season. He was a man who you really did have to worry about, whatever Don Revie told you about your own abilities. If you gave him an inch, he would finish up by taking half the field. Let your concentration slip, even for a fraction of a second, and you were in deep trouble. I know from personal experience.

'And anyone who thinks that Mr Pele wasn't able to "take it" couldn't be more wrong. He could take it all right – and he could dish it out too. It was Pele who gave me the loveliest black eye that I ever received in my footballing career.'

It was in 1966, just before the final stages of the World Cup. Scotland had failed to qualify in the preliminary stages and Brazil were in Britain finishing off their preparations for the task that lay ahead. The match with Scotland was simply a warm-up as far as the Brazilians were concerned but to the Scots it was much more than that.

166

'Our attitude could probably have been described as sour grapes in some quarters,' Billy recalled. 'Our heads were full of the fact that England had qualified and we hadn't. We realized that the match against the Brazilians was only a friendly but our attitude said "OK, this is our chance to prove that we can still have our moment of glory against the current World Cup holders." As far as we were concerned we were going to play this game to the full.'

Billy Bremner was given the job of marking Pele. Everyone knew of his skills, and everyone knew that he must be allowed no space in which to exercise them.

'I was told to stick to him like glue. Even if he went off the field for a bit of attention during the game I was to remain near the touchline so that I could be breathing down his neck when he returned. I think I did a pretty good job of marking him too. I had decided that the best way to do the job was to let him know I was there from the starting whistle. I reasoned that once he realized I was going to be on his back for the whole ninety minutes, he might think better of showing off his skills in this warm-up game and save them for the forthcoming tournament. To prove my point, the first time we went for a fifty–fifty ball, I put everything I knew into the tackle. It was fair, but hard. Very hard. In fact, I had never tackled harder in my life.

'Pele certainly got the message. He knew straight away that he had an opponent who wouldn't give him time or room to manoeuvre. This is the point when many of the so-called "greats" decide that discretion is the better part of valour and go for the easy ride. They don't really want to face up to these British-style tackles. That wasn't the case with Pele.

'He and I were not that much different in size, and I assume that the Brazilian thought the odds were probably even when it came to a test of physical strength. The next time we clashed, I was made very aware of this. The ball came over high and we went up for it together. As I rose towards the ball I could see, from the corner of my eye, Pele taking off too. I was sure that he would draw back in the final split second. The next thing that I was aware of, I was stretched out on the ground and one of my eyes had started to swell. I finished up with the biggest "shiner" I had ever had. Pele hadn't drawn back at all, he had gone for the ball with the same determination that I had – and it was me that got the worst of the encounter.

'From that moment on I had got his measure. Pele had ability – I knew that well enough even before the game had started – but the essential ingredients to go with such ability, and therefore make a player great, are pure guts and courage. I now knew that I had an opponent who had both of those things – Pele had the lot. In fact, Pele went on to show just how he had earned all those glowing reports about him. No matter how tightly I tried to mark him, he was still able to make space for himself out of virtually nothing. The situation became a personal challenge and I did my level best to keep him under control – but he still managed to demonstrate his brilliant ball control and balance, and he packed a tremendous shot in either foot. I have to say that Pele really brought it home to me that he was every bit as good as we had been led to believe. I do not believe that there has been a player anywhere, now or then, who could mark Pele so well that he would have been eliminated as a threat.'

Pele certainly convinced Bremner, who was always ready to give credit where it was due, of his ability. Bremner, however, did not have the same regard for other so-called foreign stars.

'On two occasions, both in World Cup internationals, I had the job of containing Rivera – the so-called "golden boy" of Italian football. As was the case with Pele, my job was to follow Rivera wherever he went on the park. I have to admit that he shattered me almost as much as Pele – but for an entirely different reason. Pele gave as much as he got, he couldn't be shackled, and he proved that he had courage as well as pure footballing skill. Rivera certainly had a measure of skill, but it really shook me to discover that this "golden boy" just accepted everything, including my tight marking and hard tackling. He never once tried to shake me off or try to show me that he was capable of going in hard for the ball.

'He was complacent. If I was going to be breathing down his neck for the entire ninety minutes then that was how it was going to be. Wherever he went I went and, as far as he was concerned, that just meant that he was going to have a poor game. I suppose what shook me most was the fact that he seemed to be quite content with the situation. He never once gave me the impression that he wanted even to try to turn the tables on me. His attitude made my job a lot easier, of course, but I do feel that such an attitude is totally inexcusable in a so-called star world-class footballer. I know that if I had been his manager I would have had something to say.

'The one thing that I will say in Rivera's favour – maybe it was a part of his complacency, I don't really know – was that he never once lost his temper. He accepted all the hard knocks, and he took a bit of stick from me, and never retaliated once. I don't think he said a word to me, either in Italian or English, throughout the whole 180 minutes that we were in opposition.'

Bremner liked a footballer to be a footballer and always gave praise where it was deserved. The complacent attitude of Rivera was completely alien to the volatile Scot, who expected an opponent at least to fight to the best of his ability. He was convinced that most famous foreign players could not measure up to home-grown British talent, though there were a few notable exceptions in addition to Pele.

'I would class Florian Albert as a talented player. He was certainly able to score goals and he was extremely deceptive once he latched on to a ball. He would have you relaxing because of his ability to hide his striking power behind an apparently casual exterior. He had class and could have been a lot better if he had been willing to put more "bite" and effort into his play. He often kept out of it for much of the ninety minutes but, when he did decide to go, it was all hands on deck. Most of the time, though, he didn't really need checking out because he didn't get into the game enough.

'His team-mate, Varga, was in a different category altogether. Varga would weigh up a situation and seemed able to see things much more quickly than most players whom I came up against. In fact, he compared fairly favourably with Pele in my eyes. He could create moves, read the game well – and stick the ball in the net. If I had to compare Pele and Varga on what I saw of them, I would say that Pele had the edge because he was more consistent. For sure, Varga was world class – and he could certainly get stuck in. There was one occasion when we both went for the ball together. Neither of us held back, even at that last vital split second. I kept going and Varga kept coming – and he won the fight. I hated losing the ball at any time, and so I snarled at him as I often did when I was excited. Having won the ball, and just as swiftly parted with it, Varga laughed in my face and simply walked away. It really needled me at the time but, looking back, I wish that I had been able to do the same thing on many other occasions when I retaliated to someone else's temper. Varga's response to my temperamental outburst was exactly the right attitude that a player should adopt, and it is an essential part of the make-up of a top-class professional footballer. My own trouble was that I was never able to keep my big mouth shut often enough – I should have taken lessons from Varga!

'We met the Hungarian team Ujpesti Dosza twice in the Inter-Cities Fairs Cup. Bene, of course, was in that team. When we met at Elland Road for the first time they did nothing against us and I began to think that all the hype about the Hungarians was nothing after all. In the return game in Budapest, however, it was a far different story. Yes, we drew 1–1 on that occasion, but if the result had reflected the way that the Hungarian team played, the scoreline would have read 6–1 in their favour. In that match they were the greatest team that I ever encountered – and I've come up against quite a few in the past. They ran us ragged and it was as if we were chasing shadows. They had four shots which shook the woodwork before they finally scored just before half-time. After the break they came at us as if they wanted to run us into the ground. They almost succeeded too. We were gasping for breath, we were leg weary – and I'll never know how we managed to survive.

'They came at us in one attack and the ball whacked the bar of our goal and, while they were excitedly appealing that the ball had bounced down over the goal-line, we played to the whistle which hadn't been blown. The result was that we broke away and Peter Lorimer stuck the ball into their net. Unlike the Hungarian attempt, that goal counted. From then on the game was a real hard-luck story for Ujpesti Dosza. It wasn't a case of bad finishing on their part either. They made the openings, hit the ball well, but the ball would not go in the net. I have to admit that I felt a little sorry for Bene on that occasion. At Elland Road he had been no different from the rest of his team-mates: pretty good, but nothing really to worry about. But in Budapest he ran the legs off us. He fought for the ball, he worked, he skimmed down the wing and beat man after man, he caused havoc whenever he got within striking distance. If he wasn't sending over dangerous centres, he was cutting inside and letting fly with shots that went like bullets from a gun. Managing to get that draw was a miracle.

'They showed how good they were when we met them for the second time at Elland Road. In that game, they scored the only goal of the match – which knocked us out of the Fairs Cup on that occasion. I could well understand how the Hungarians came over and defeated England at Wembley in 1953. They became the first continental team to win on English soil when they defeated England 6–3. I can only think that they must have played like Ujpesti Dosza did in Budapest when we met them – the only difference being that on the Wembley occasion, all the shots went in!'

Spain boasted a team which gave Leeds United a real problem in the Inter-Cities Fairs Cup play-off in 1966. Real Zaragoza fielded a great forward line which had been christened 'The Magnificent Five' by the fans and the press. Bremner hardly rated them, but admitted that they lived up to their reputation on that particular occasion.

'We'd all heard about this "Magnificent Five", especially Villa,' said Billy. 'He disappointed me actually and I wouldn't have rated him as in the top class. The rest of their forward line weren't that good either, even though they did give us a walloping in the play-off. They scored three really good goals against us inside the first quarter of an hour. I have to admit that they did play some magnificent stuff during the early part of the match.

'You would think that three goals like that would kill off any team, wouldn't you? But not Leeds United. Whatever our faults as a team, we were not quitters. We fought and we fought every inch of the way and tried our best to pull those goals back. Real Zaragoza did the opposite. With those three goals they should have kept going and made it six, but instead they "died". Instead of grinding us into the ground, they failed to keep up the pressure when they had such an advantage. It's not just sour grapes because they won anyway, but again a European team showed a distinct lack of the killer instinct.'

Bremner classed British players in the top bracket of world soccer. In his opinion, the best forward line that he ever came up against belonged to an English team – West Ham. The occasion was a League Cup tie when West Ham and Leeds United came out of the hat together.

'In those days we didn't go in for heavy defeats – if Leeds United lost by more than a goal or two, it became headline news. So when a forward line pumped seven goals into our net, it went to show what a great set of forwards they were. West Ham's attack on us was little short of fantastic.

'Poor old Dave Harvey was standing in for Gary Sprake in that tie and, how ever he tried to save those goals, it made no difference. The West Ham forwards couldn't put a foot wrong. Dave actually did save us from a much heavier defeat and he certainly could not be blamed for any of the goals that went past him. It was almost like a coconut shy where every ball won a coconut. Dave Harvey was lucky to escape with his life, so lethal were those Hammers shots!'

Other star players in Britain during Bremner's days at Elland Road included members of his own team. He rated Johnny Giles as a player with one of the shrewdest brains in football.

'Johnny joined us from Manchester United. He looked so meek and mild I began to wonder if he would be able to stand up to the strain of life at Elland Road. I already knew quite a bit about him, of course. He had been at Old Trafford since he was fifteen, he was Irish and quite a clever footballer. He had even won an FA Cup medal with Manchester United but he had never been a regular first-teamer. Some people said that he was too nice to make the top-class grade and, at the time, even I wasn't sure how he would fit into the Leeds set-up, where everyone had to chase and work and graft and, to be blunt, get stuck in.

'I soon discovered that Johnny had this great built-in determination. Johnny himself had decided that Manchester United was not the team for him and, when Leeds came in for him, that was that. I think that he was determined from the start to prove that Leeds United's gain was a definite loss for Manchester United. Johnny was always after the ball, always looking for it – and when he got it, his natural shrewdness helped him use it to the best advantage. He proved the point that he could be compared with any footballer of his time. I have to say that when I saw him out on the field, I was always glad that he was on our side.'

Other stars of the British football scene of Bremner's day included Jimmy Greaves, Denis Law and Bobby Charlton. Billy had something to say about all of them.

'Jimmy Greaves was a player with a great scoring flair. Good though he undoubtedly was, I have to say that I would rather play against him than against someone like Denis Law. Greaves, though, seemed to be a real hoodoo on Leeds United. Whenever we met Tottenham, Greaves always managed to stick one in our net. He only ever needed a few inches of space in which to work. If you gave him half a chance he would grab a goal.

'If Greaves was playing, Don Revie would always warn us, "Make him go to his right – at least that way you'll make it a bit more difficult for him." On one occasion at White Hart Lane, we were playing to this instruction and it seemed to be doing the trick. Then one of our defenders forgot for the merest fraction of a second. Up to that moment Jimmy Greaves had been kept under control, but in that split second he had spotted the smallest of gaps, and the ball was in the back of our net.'

Why, then, did Bremner say that he would prefer playing against Greaves than he would against Law?

'Denis Law would go straight in wherever there was trouble. He was no fool, but he'd go right in and get his boot to the ball. I have no hesitation in saying that Denis was the most complete footballer in the world – including Pele. He was so quick in the strike and his deadliness came from his anticipation of when the ball could be won.

'His speed, anticipation, control, brilliance in heading a ball, his ability to leap like a stag, all made him a dangerous opponent, and he had two good feet which made him a deadly marksman too. In short, he had the lot.

'Denis had a team-mate at Manchester United who was equally courageous, equally adept at creating scoring situations – although in a slightly different manner. His name was George Best. He was the most fantastic player I have ever seen for stopping and changing direction, with the ball completely under control, while travelling at top speed. Without doubt, he was one of the best, if not the best, dribbler in the game. You knew what he was going to do, but there was nothing you could about stopping him when he was on form. And he usually was on form. He was a natural entertainer too and, of course, the footballing public loved him. He was very much his own man and he was great as a player.

'Another great British player who I would put in the same bracket as the fabulous Pele is Bobby Charlton. Some people said that Bobby Charlton didn't exactly go in for the ball like a Billy Bremner or a Dave Mackay, and that he wasn't particularly brave when it came to heading the ball. He did score one great goal with his head, though, and that goal helped Manchester United towards a triumph in the European Cup.

'I think that Bobby Charlton was a soccer artist. I could have watched him play all day. His changes of pace and direction were phenomenal, and many a goalkeeper was able to vouch for the fact that both feet were packed with power and accuracy.

'Don Revie probably brought it to our attention that Bobby Charlton meant a little more than our usual opposition. He didn't say anything about leaving our opponents to do the worrying when Bobby was going to be in action. His orders were always very much to the point and one of the most significant points was, "Cut out Bobby Charlton, and we're halfway to success." Bobby was so often the mainspring of any Manchester United attack. He would collect the ball, vary his pace and direction, and start to spray the passes around with such accuracy that George Best or Denis Law were away on an attacking foray.

'Whatever he did, Bobby Charlton spelt danger to his opponents. Don Revie made a special point when he reminded us about him before a game. And that, coming from Don Revie, was just about the highest tribute he could pay to anyone who was not a Leeds United player.'

Bremner was often asked for his opinion of the Leeds United side of more recent years, especially the squad which won the League championship in 1992.

'Some excellent players came through from the youth squad. Apart from David Batty, I rate Gary Speed and the even younger ones like Andy Gray, Gary Kelly and Noel Whelan who went to Coventry. Howard Wilkinson also made some excellent signings like Gary McAllister, Gordon Strachan and Eric Cantona. All three of these had a tremendous influence on the side.

'I find it difficult to compare the sides of today with those in which I played because the circumstances and the game itself have changed. I have seen the modern Leeds play some great football, but I have also seen them play some terrible football. I know that we had our off-days too, but they were fairly isolated cases. We did not often go through long spells without scoring goals. A lot of people say that we were totally defensive; that is completely untrue. We played a free-flowing, attacking game but happened to have a cast-iron defence as well.

'I was delighted when Leeds won the championship in 1992 but they seemed to lose their way after that. If I have to stop sitting on the fence and being tactful, I would have to say that, although Leeds were the best in the land in 1992, as a team they would not have lived with either of the championship sides of my playing days.'

16

A WILL TO WIN

Leeds once played eight matches in eighteen days, which is tough going, especially when you consider the travelling, preparation and, of course, training. While others may have been exhausted, Billy Bremner appeared to thrive on such physical and mental pressure. As he once said: 'Keep winning and you don't feel the strain.

'It is a fact that anyone involved in a profession with a lot of stress will suffer from some ailment or other,' said Billy. 'Football is no exception. There has always been an outcry about the amount of football that the leading clubs have to cram into a season. Their players are not only involved in more League matches than the professional players of Europe, they can also expect to be called on for long runs in domestic, as well as European, cup competitions.

'It is not just the short-term effects that worry managers. Certainly some pretty drastic developments can take place in a matter of days. Leeds United were aware of that only too well. Just look back at what happened to our assault on soccer's greatest treble. At the time it seemed to be well within our grasp, and yet, because we had to cram so many matches into such a short time, we came away with nothing.'

The following year Everton took Leeds' place in the European Cup competition and Bremner gave them full credit for their skill. He also pointed out that they faced the same problems, even though they did their best to avoid them.

'Everton won the League title from us on merit. I have to say that they were worthy successors to us as English champions. Even if we had been at top strength we would have found it extremely difficult to overhaul them because they played so magnificently during the run-in.

'However, they soon learned that there was a price to pay – even though they tried to avoid some of the problems that we had had to face. They did not enter the League Cup competition that season in an effort to cut out some of the pressure that had added to our own problems.'

Everton found that, despite their attempts to alleviate any extra strain, the demands made on their players were proving to be overwhelming. Within three months of the start of the season Everton's manager, Harry Catterick, felt that he had to speak out.

'We are having to make too many demands on our top players,' he complained. 'With an almost non-stop round of commitments, we are making the British professional the hardest-working footballer in the world. If it continues to go on this way the strain could become intolerable!'

Bremner knew exactly what he meant.

'Harry Catterick was quite right when he said that. There was never the time for a player to recover from an injury when one important match followed another within three or four days. Even forty-eight hours can make a tremendous difference to a key player's fitness.

'It was never the case of too much football, though. It was the sort of football in which this class of player was involved. There are always a lot of tension games. In the top division there are never any easy games – almost every match is like a Cup tie. Even when you are playing at home, you still have to overcome the problem of breaking down a packed defence. How many teams go away and play attacking football?

'I suppose it has never been proved that these gluts of fixtures have done anything to shorten playing careers. That would depend upon so many different factors. No, that side of the question depends very much upon each individual and there have always been some pretty resilient characters about.

178

Nowadays, too, there isn't the same need for players to burn themselves out as they did in the past. Football has become much more of a team game than it ever was. Everybody is doing their fair share of the running and that makes it much easier to keep going on.

'In the old days, too, there were a lot of great personalities and characters who used to impose their authority on a match. Without those characters there has to be a great deal more teamwork to compensate. That is a big thing to remember when you are talking about stresses and strains.

'I'm sure that it must have been a lot harder for those great characters like Roy Paul and Len Shackleton to turn on their human dynamos for match after match than it is for modern players. We still do have a few characters, of course. In my own day it was George Best for one and wee Alan Ball for another. However, whatever characters there are now, by and large the burden on any particular individual isn't as heavy as it used to be.'

Teamwork may well have changed some of the problems of concentrated games, but it is not just the physical effort involved that is so tiring. In today's high-profile game, the mental effort and pressure involved in playing important matches is even more exhausting. Billy Bremner was well aware of that problem too.

'Some people used to say that it should be easy for us to play, even at top level, two matches a week. They were probably thinking only of the physical side of the game. Well, if it were only the matter of going out and playing like amateurs do on a Saturday afternoon, it would be quite easy to get through even the most congested programme. What many people seem to forget is the mental side of the picture.

'At Leeds we used to say that you should come off the park mentally as well as physically tired. The tension and worry used to start even before the game, then through the game you had to be thinking all the time of the problems connected with it. Nowadays the game has got even more high profile and the mental strain that goes with that is even more pronounced.'

179

Injury, or its possibility, is another cause for stress. Few players emerge unscathed by the end of their careers and the
congested fixtures caused by the increased competitions for
top-class teams make injury a real possibility as exhaustion
takes it effect.

'I was one of the luckier ones when it came to injuries,' said
Bremner. 'But I am well aware of how much they get you
down. They are always depressing. You have to come back to
the club morning and afternoon for treatment and there is
nothing lonelier than that little back room. Even if you have a
couple of team-mates with you, that old routine of going
through the same remedial circuits every session just grinds
you down.

'I don't think that the game has got any harder, even though
there is so much more at stake these days. If you look back
through the records you will see that there have always been
injuries. People talk about hard players today, but I think there
were much harder players in the game a few years back.'

Bremner wasn't convinced that it was the number of games
that a footballer played that caused him to get over-fatigued.
He put it down to a much more simple reason.

A player only starts to worry about getting tired when the
results start to go against him. I know this is true from my own
experience.

'In 1967, Leeds played eight matches in the space of only
eighteen days, and some of that time was taken up by flying
to Italy and back. That mammoth slog didn't worry us a bit.
Of course, we might not have felt quite so casual about it if
we had known from the start just what lay ahead of us. Two
of those games were just thrown in as we went along because
we had to meet Sunderland three times before we finally
knocked them out of the FA Cup. In fact we had to take a
reserve team with us to Hull. They stood by in case they had
to fly out to Italy and play a Fairs Cup tie in Bologna. It
almost came to that, too, because another replay seemed
likely before we finally settled that serial with the men from
Roker Park.

'Those three Cup ties, followed by a goalless draw with Manchester City in a League game, took it out of us, though, and we lost to Bologna in Italy. However, we had tied on aggregate scores and with my luck we won the flip of the disc and got through to the next round. Then we flew back home and won all three of our Easter matches – one at Blackpool and two against Sheffield United.

'We felt good because success breeds success and when you are winning you feel that you can go on playing for ever. If we had been beaten in three of those first six games we would have been really dead beat by the time we faced the last two, because we would not have been feeling positive and looking forward to playing them.

'It shows how the mental approach can make such a big difference. The last five of those games were played in the space of eight days and yet we were still fresh enough, mentally as well as physically, to smack in eight goals during the last three games with only one scored against us. We were high on success.'

Travelling must be one of the most tiring things about football. In this country a team can travel the day before a match and therefore count on a good night's sleep before the game. Travelling and playing abroad is often a different story, as Billy Bremner remembered.

'When you are abroad it is often difficult to get to sleep after a match. Sometimes it would be well after two in the morning and I would still be trying to get off to sleep. Then, when we finally had to get up after perhaps just three or four hours' rest, we had to face the flight back home. Getting home wasn't the end of it either. We'd have about twenty-four hours to recharge our batteries before the next match and, if it was an away match, we'd be travelling again only hours after getting off the plane.'

Despite all the energy expended on the potential glories of the continent, Billy Bremner never thought the competitions a waste of time. This is what he had to say on the subject.

'Whatever the problems – and I think we all know that there can be a few – being in Europe is very good for clubs. On the financial front it always did a lot towards paying the wages for a club like Leeds.

'My years of battling in Europe did nothing to take the edge off my appetite for football. I have to admit that I always enjoyed the close season when it arrived but, by the time three weeks or so had passed, I, like most other footballers, I'm sure, would be thirsting to get back into action.

'I know there are times when a player might feel that he could well do with a mid-season break but that might not be the best thing for him to do. As a case in point, look at what happened to Terry Cooper.

'Terry played in forty-eight competitive games for Leeds and then he went on to Mexico with the England team for the World Cup. Early the next season, our manager, Don Revie, wanted to give him a rest in an easy Fairs Cup game against a Norwegian side. As it happened, several other players were carrying injuries and so Terry had to soldier on and play. After all that, Terry was in such brilliant form a few weeks later that he became the first winner of a national Player of the Week award.

'It all goes to show that as long as you are doing well you want to be out there playing, and the better you do, the longer you can go on.'

Bremner was a firm believer in the theory that if you are in a good frame of mind you will be more successful, but he also rated very highly the part that supporters play in their club's feelgood factor, or indeed the part opposing supporters can play in fazing the visiting side. There were few grounds more daunting than Anfield, for instance, with its famous Kop – even today, with seating installed.

'They are devoted to their own team, Liverpool, but they'll give credit where credit is due – whether it is the Reds or their opponents. They showed that when we clinched the League title there.

'I should really refer to the Kop in the singular because, although thousands of fans congregate there and they have this wonderful sense of humour and an understanding that is almost telepathic, they all sound as one in their appreciation of the game and good football.

'On one occasion while playing there, Gary Sprake scored a goal against himself. He had picked up the ball and drew back his arm to throw it to one of our defenders. Suddenly the ball slipped from his fingers and rolled across his own goal-line. Gary's expression of agony changed to one of absolute horror when he realized what had happened, especially when the Kop, true to form, began to take up the tune "Careless Hands". Even Gary finished up laughing. He didn't laugh during the interval, however, when the Anfield disc jockey put that same record on the turntable to the joy of the Kop and the other Liverpool supporters! Gary felt that was rubbing it in too much.

'It was just one of those things for Gary, but he was never allowed to forget it. Supporters or your own mind can make or break you. At Elland Road in my day, both made us.'

17

BREMNER – THE MAN

Having been brought up in a typical Scottish family household, Bremner himself became a doting family man with a wife he obviously loved very deeply, a son, two daughters and a grandson – each of whom had a special place in his heart.

It was a Friday night at the Plaza in Stirling when Billy and Vicky first saw each other. The Plaza was the local dance hall, a kind of no-man's land where people from either side of the water could meet and lay down their ground rules for life. Issy McDonald was at the Plaza that night and was powdering her nose when a flushed Vicky entered the ladies' room.

'She looked a little pleased with herself,' said Issy. 'We guessed that she'd met someone, so we started to ask the sort of questions that girls ask. Vicky admitted that she had met and danced with a lad she liked the look of but that she was a bit worried about him. "I think he's giving me a bit of a tale," she said. "He's told me that he plays football for Leeds United and that he's got a car!" "Aye," I replied. "He's telling you the truth. That's Billy Bremner, he's a pal of mine and he is with Leeds United and he does have a car."'

Alex Smith was also there that night.

'Friday night was the big night for us. Billy used to come home as often as he could and if it happened to be a Friday, we always went to the Plaza. They used to have bands and groups in those days. Every Friday it was "Lulu and the Luvvers"; Lulu was just making a name for herself in those days. It probably doesn't sound all that romantic, but when Billy met Vicky for the first time at the Plaza, Lulu and the Luvvers, and the rest of us just disappeared into the background. Cupid scored a brilliant goal. I met Vicky's pal, Ann, but Cupid put that one over the bar.'

The rest of the story really belongs to Vicky herself.

'I went home and told my parents that I had met this lad. When I told them a bit more about him they nearly collapsed. It wasn't because it was Billy Bremner, or that he played football for Leeds. He was from Raploch, an area which was known locally as "Chicago". They said that his car was probably stolen. The rest of Stirling looked upon Raploch as the sort of place that you would never admit to coming from. Needless to say, they were not impressed.'

Billy was already homesick down in England but, after meeting Vicky, he was even more drawn to Stirling and talked to Alex Smith about the possibility of getting a transfer to Stirling Albion.

'I told him that he would be crazy even to think about it,' said Alex. 'I explained that, while there was nothing wrong with Stirling Albion for someone like myself, he was in the best place in the world for someone with his talent. I was only a part-timer, like most Scottish footballers. I had to get up early and go to work and then fit my training into evenings or the occasional afternoon off. I kept reminding Billy of that every time he started getting homesick – which was near enough every day.'

When Billy returned home on his frequent trips, he liked to have parties for his pals. They were simple affairs with the strongest drink being his favourite limeade. The friends used to chat, have a snack and a soft drink and play music, or perhaps have a sing-song.

'Billy loved that. He liked to have his friends around him,' said Issy McDonald. 'He didn't have time for hangers-on. He liked to have near enough the same group of folk with whom he'd grown up. He could let himself relax with his pals and he would forget all about his career at these times. When the time came for him to drive back to Leeds he often did not want to go. I used to tell him that he had far too much talent not to go. He owed it to himself, to his club, and his country, to do as well as he could in the game. I had been a fan of his since he started playing for the school team and I just knew he was good enough to really make it. I didn't want to see him throw it all away.'

Meanwhile Billy and Vicky kept in touch and saw each other whenever he paid visits to Stirling.

'He invited me to one of the gatherings in Raploch, but I declined. I don't think I had the nerve to tell my parents that I was going to a party in Raploch – they would probably have locked me up for the night. Billy kept on asking and so I eventually agreed and became one of his circle of friends.'

Alex Smith watched the developments from a safe distance.

'Vicky and Billy were an ideal match. They were both young and innocent in a way; Vicky much more innocent than Bill, of course. She knew little of the world outside Stirling, and I don't really think she wanted to know much about it until she took a liking to Billy – then her interest extended as far as Leeds. I'm not sure that she was aware of just how much she meant to Billy until Don Revie paid her a visit and told her.'

Vicky recalled that visit.

'He did not just tell me about Billy and his progress and what he thought about his prospects, he also told me all about Leeds United and his own ambitions for the club. He talked to me about his plans for Billy's involvement with the exciting future of Leeds United and how difficult it was getting through to Billy to make him understand what a great future he would have – if he would only shake off his homesickness and dedicate himself to his career and his club. Don told me that Billy would be doing himself a disservice if he didn't get on with his career in the best possible way. He told me a bit about Leeds and Yorkshire as well, and then he left me to think about everything that he had said.

'I did think about it, too, and for Billy's sake it all made sense to me. I don't know if I was including myself in all this at the time, but the more I talked to Billy, and gave him my opinion of what he should be doing about his career, the more it became obvious that we were discussing our future and not just his. The next thing we knew we were talking about getting married. We were still in our teens, yet that didn't seem to matter. It seemed right and we knew we could make a go of it.'

Alex Smith was Billy's best man on their wedding day, 14 November 1961.

'It was a good wedding, very Scottish and very much a family affair. The young couple looked good – at least Vicky did! On the morning of the wedding, Billy and I went for a haircut. We were cropped a bit closer than we wanted and he and I agreed, when we looked at the photographs later, that we both looked like a couple of skinned rabbits. It was a very happy day, though, and the start of a very happy marriage.

'I had to admire how Vicky adapted to her new way of life. She supported Billy throughout and yet she was as homesick as he was. This young girl was suddenly transported from the quiet backwaters of the more sedentary area of Stirling into the hustle and bustle of the city of Leeds. Her friends and family were all back in Scotland and her husband was out much of the time, either training or playing – sometimes at the other end of the country. She did very well to cope with life in that situation.'

Issy McDonald saw the relationship from both sides.

'I can remember Vicky asking me about Billy, but I remember Billy asking me about Vicky as well. His eyes lit up when I told him that she had recently won a beauty queen contest. I watched them settle down together and continued to follow Billy's career, even though I was posted abroad after joining the army. We lost touch, but I used to read every scrap of news about Billy and Vicky and I was delighted that they had a happy marriage. I guessed that they would. It's almost a tradition for at least one guest at a wedding to say, "They were made for each other." In Billy and Vicky's case it was absolutely true.'

The young couple lived in a house provided by Leeds

United when they were first married. Some years later they moved to the village near Doncaster where Vicky still lives.

'It was very hard for me to get used to living in Leeds,' said Vicky. 'I was not really interested in football and so I didn't go to watch the games very often. The other wives tended to meet up at the club and make an afternoon of it, but I preferred to stay at home. I was not anti-social, but I suppose that I was a bit shy. We lived at Temple Newsham, which was not a bad area, but I never felt the need to go out a lot. My main interest was my husband. If Billy was happy, I was happy.'

After a few years their first child was born – a boy, also named Billy.

'Billy was thrilled to bits,' said Vicky. 'He was a very proud dad and he was an excellent father. He liked to be involved with all the nappy changing and those chores that are not the best part of being a parent. A couple of years later Donna came along and then, four years after that, the family was completed with the birth of Amanda. He loved each one of them and enjoyed his family very much. He would do anything for them, and when Chad – Amanda's son – came along, Billy doted on being a grandfather.

'Chad became known as Billy's shadow. They spent every possible moment together. Billy was always a great one for pulling the children's legs – and anyone else's come to that. He had a fantastic sense of humour and the house was always full of laughter when he was at home. Donna tried to reverse it on him once when she bought Chad a full replica kit for Manchester United. When Chad turned up wearing it, Billy shook his head and said, "I can't pick you up Chad, I'll burn my hands!" If Chad ever mentioned Manchester United, Billy used to pretend that he was going to be sick. It was all in fun, of course. Billy was a great practical joker. It was not unusual for him to hide behind a door and frighten the life out of you when you walked into the room. He used to do things like that all his life, not just in the early years. He could drive you crazy at times.'

Although he was comfortable in South Yorkshire, Billy never

neglected the folks back home, and if his travels took him anywhere near Stirling, he would always drop in to see his family and friends.

'He enjoyed coming back to see everyone,' said Issy McDonald. 'And there was many a chap who has had some money stuffed into his hand if Billy thought he could do with it. He never made a big deal of it. He would just quietly take something out of his pocket and hand it over as discreetly as he could. He used to talk to the youngsters and encourage them as well. He always did his best for the various charities, too, and he was greatly admired by everyone in the area. The people of Stirling have always been immensely proud of him.

'When Billy heard that the Raploch boys team needed some help while he was manager of Doncaster he sent a complete set of team strip, a match ball, and various other bits and pieces. It was all greatly appreciated in Raploch and was typical of Billy's generosity and concern for others.'

Alex Smith remembers a time when Billy's generosity nearly backfired.

'Billy was playing in a Cup Final at Wembley and he arranged a couple of tickets for me. I had been to his house in Leeds many times and he suggested that he leave the tickets at the house so that we could travel down, let ourselves in, stay if we wanted, pick up the tickets and then head for Wembley. It all made perfect sense and Billy told us where he would hide the keys.

'The plan was perfect until we actually arrived at the house. Billy had not left the keys. I knew Billy well enough to know that he had probably forgotten; he had a terrible memory for arrangements. I also knew that there was a window that was always loose and, another thing that I knew about Billy, that it would remain loose for as long as it was up to him to fix it. I went to the window and, sure enough, I could open it and squeeze in.

'It wasn't long before the police arrived. I opened the door from the inside and they wanted to know who I was and what my pal and I were doing inside someone else's house. I explained that we had come to pick up the tickets and showed them to the two police officers. I think they grew even more suspicious then. Billy had not left a note or anything and they refused to believe my story. Then I had a brainwave and told them that if they would allow me to search out Billy's wedding photographs, they would see me on them as Billy's best man.

'It took some time but we eventually found them and pointed to Billy and myself. The two policemen studied my face, looked at the photograph, studied my face again and then burst into laughter. It was the haircuts that they found so amusing – mine was the worst. However, that seemed to clinch it and they were happy with my story. I saw Billy later and he found the whole episode funny, not realizing that his memory lapse could have caused my pal and I not only to miss the Cup Final but to spend the night in police custody. He might just as well have said, "Well, that'll teach you to be more careful in future." It was typical of the great guy.'

If Billy Bremner knew that he was in the wrong, he would be the first to apologize, but he was a bad loser . . . very bad.

'He was a terrible loser,' said Vicky. 'If his team lost, even in a game that did not mean very much, he took it very personally. He just hated to lose. Even when he played games with the children, he would never let them win, unless it was on merit. That was partly to give them an edge, but it was also because he just did not like to lose at anything.

'If he was injured, or suspended, and could not play, he was like a bear with a sore head. He lived for the game. Even when he couldn't play, he still went round to the ground to be involved. His favourite days of any week were Wednesday and Saturday, when it would be most likely that he would be playing in a match. Apart from his family, his football was all that mattered to him.

'He regretted stopping playing when he did. He always said that he would retire when he was thirty-five, and when the time came he didn't really hesitate. He knew that it wasn't going to get any easier and that there were a few injuries which took a little longer to get over, so he decided to stop. A few years later he wished that he had kept going for just a little bit longer. He felt he could have played for another season or two before going into management full time.

'He enjoyed being a manager mostly, I think, because he enjoyed the coaching. He took the job very seriously and there were times when I wished that he would take it a little easier. At Leeds, for instance, he was out night after night travelling all over the place looking at players, looking at opponents, trying to find new talent, keeping the supporters happy. It was a tremendous stress. He was very proud of nearly getting Leeds back into the First Division and to the Cup Final in the same year. He loved the club and it was a real blow to him when he was sacked. He felt sure that he was going to get them back into the First Division before long and he had made all his plans accordingly. When they sacked him it was like chopping his legs away from him. He was touched by all the good wishes from the supporters.

'After he finished at Doncaster for the second time, I prayed that nobody else would offer him a job as manager. He put far too much of himself into the job and I always felt that it was a pretty thankless task. I didn't like to see him get as tired out as he did.'

Vicky's prayers were answered, of course.

After his direct involvement with the game was over, Billy lost none of his love of it. He was still a regular spectator at Elland Road and often went there with one of his greatest friends, Allan Clarke.

'Billy and I became pals when we roomed together while we were at Leeds. He was always full of fun and became so close a friend that he was really like a brother to me. Our families also became close. Billy was a one-off, a unique character. I've never met anyone else like him. As a player, he had no equal, and I have never met anyone with such all-consuming passion for the game.

'If we ever lost a game our dressing room was like a morgue. Billy was as quiet, if not quieter, than anyone. He was not the sort who went around kicking things, he just sat quietly –

191

thinking his own thoughts. It was never more evident than when we won the FA Cup on 1972 and then, two days later, went to Wolves to try to clinch the championship. We were elated after the win at Wembley and nobody was noisier than Billy. Some forty-eight hours later, the FA Cup was forgotten and we were devastated at having failed in our championship bid. Nobody was more subdued than Billy.

'I think one of his proudest moments was winning the FA Cup. He took immense pleasure and pride from receiving the trophy. Quite often, when a captain has lifted the trophy, he passes it to the next player and so on. Billy didn't do that. We were talking about it not long before he died and he said, "I just didn't want to let go of it. I had always wanted to hold it." It was so typical of him, winning meant so much to him.

'He was also very passionate about playing for Scotland. He loved it. I never knew this at the time, but Don Revie probably stopped me from winning more than nineteen caps for England. He used to phone the England manager and say, "I'm sorry, Alf, the boy's had a knock so I'm not sending him." Billy apparently heard about this and told the boss never to interfere with his appearances for Scotland. He said that if Revie ever tried to stop him going, he would just go anyway. He told Don that to his face, too.

'Billy was also proud of the time that Leeds won the championship for the second time. It wasn't so much the championship as the fact that we went twenty-nine games without defeat. That prompted Bill Shankly to say that if someone didn't beat us by Christmas we might as well be presented with the championship there and then. It was quite a tribute from Shankly and meant a lot to us all, but especially to Billy who had such great admiration for him.

'I think the moment that he really enjoyed the most was when Leeds clinched their first championship while playing away at Liverpool. The whole of Anfield rose and applauded them and Billy never forgot that. He often talked about it as a great example of what the game should be about, rivalry, but with mutual respect and friendship.

'There's another thing about Billy Bremner that people probably wouldn't appreciate unless they had actually lived with him. He loved to sing. Any excuse for a song and Billy was first in the queue. He used to sing while he was shaving and while he was in the bath or shower. I used to play a trick on him and he never realized it. When we were room-mates he always used to take the first bath and he would sing at the top of his voice. Then I would take a bath and he would still be singing, so I used to start whistling something entirely different and, without realizing it, he would begin singing whatever I was whistling. I'd even change the tune now and again and he would still follow it in song. If you asked him what he was singing he really had to think about it – he just hadn't noticed that the song had changed.

'That didn't stop when we retired. We used to take family holidays together and, just a couple of months before he died, we were all in a villa in the Algarve. I was in our bathroom and I heard Billy singing next door. I began to whistle and he immediately changed his song. I had a chuckle about that because he never did realize that I led him from song to song.

'I don't know how much he missed playing. When we went to Elland Road to see matches we would often be questioned by supporters. Their favourite question was to ask whether or not we missed it all. I always said that I did, but Billy used to shake his head and say that he didn't. He would say, "No, I had my day and I enjoyed every minute of it. It's time for someone else now." I don't know if that was how he really felt or if he was really trying to convince himself. I do know that whether or not he missed football, the game certainly missed him – yet no more than my family and I have.'

Alex Smith believed that Bremner was a realist and knew that his day had been and had gone.

'Billy realized that his level of performance had gone and he did not want to lower his personal standards. He was keen to get into management with a small club, but he wanted to end his playing days while he was still a capable footballer. He took great pride in his profession, most especially when he played for Scotland. When he was banned he was deeply upset. He told me what had happened, and it really was nothing. The media, for some reason known only to themselves, blew the whole episode way out of proportion, and the Scottish Football Association were forced to take some dramatic action. I personally believe that Billy would have achieved at least seventy-five caps but for that ban. Billy never made a public scene out of it. He knew that the SFA were in a difficult position, and he also knew that it was chiefly the press who had made something out of nothing. He was upset about the whole incident but he mostly blamed the press for their over-the-top reporting of what actually was a non-event.'

Bremner's total devotion to his country never faltered. He became as big a Scotland fan after he retired as he had been a big-hearted player when he wore the Scotland shirt.

'He used to love being at Scotland matches,' said Alex Smith. 'I remember him asking me to get tickets for the Euro 96 match with England at Wembley. I told him, "You're in the Hall of Fame and you can get as many tickets as you want," but he told me that he wanted to go in among the fans. I got him the tickets and he went with his daughter Donna, who had never been to such a game before.

'Billy was just delighted to be there. At half-time Scotland were drawing 0–0 and everyone was in great spirits. Billy took this big Scotland flag off a fan and started waving it. When the whole place started going mad for fifteen minutes, Billy was right in the middle of it, waving this massive flag.

'That was him. He loved Scotland. He may well have lived in Yorkshire but, like a lot of people who leave their homeland, he became even more committed to his country. Scotland has had a lot of great skippers but, in my eyes, he was the best ever!'

Another insight into Billy Bremner the man was the time that Leeds were travelling back from a European match in Barcelona. The party had all boarded the aircraft to take them back home when Jimmy Armfield, the manager, noticed that he was a player short. A quick head count established that it was Billy Bremner who was missing. The manager returned to the terminal where he found Billy, wearing a huge sombrero, entertaining a group of about a dozen Spanish children. Hours earlier he had been a tough guy leading the campaign on the football pitch, now here he was clowning around with a bunch of kids.

Billy Bremner never lost touch with reality. He cared about people. Whenever his travels took him to one of the world's poorer countries he always returned a wiser man – grateful for his family and his lot in life. On the football pitch he cared for nothing but victory – off it, he was a warm human being with a twinkle in his eye, a song in his heart and a kind word for everyone.

18

FINAL WHISTLE

To say that it was a shock to hear of the death of Billy Bremner, on 7 December 1997, would be an understatement. I had spoken to him only a week or two earlier and he had been as cheerful as usual – although he said that he had been going through a cold. The draw for the World Cup finals in France had just taken place and the Scotland manager, Craig Brown, took time after the draw in Marseilles to check out training camps for his team. Having done that he flew back to Scotland on the day that Billy's death was announced.

'I was shocked to hear of Billy's death,' said the Scotland boss. 'I heard the news on the radio and I was stunned. I then received numerous phone calls from the press requesting tributes to Billy and I was more than pleased to talk about him – although I wish the circumstances had been different. I had previously had the privilege of writing the foreword for Billy's book, *Scottish Football Heroes*. I had appreciated that chance and it meant even more when I heard that he had died. I had been able to make a tribute to the great wee man while he was still alive.

'Billy Bremner was a one-off, never seen before or since. A lot of people talk about what they were doing when President Kennedy died, but I shall always remember that I was returning from the draw for the 1998 World Cup when Billy Bremner died. It was a very sad day and I shall always remember it as the day when Scotland lost a national hero.'

Billy had been feeling ill at a dinner a few days before his death. On medical advice he agreed to go into Doncaster Royal Infirmary, though in truth he would have preferred to have taken a couple of aspirins and gone to bed. He always treated illnesses like he treated injuries – not to be taken too seriously. It was while he was in the Doncaster Royal Infirmary that his pneumonia was diagnosed and no amount of medical expertise could cure him. The world was then given the shocking news.

Who would have ever thought that Billy Bremner, renowned for having one of the biggest and strongest hearts in the history of football, would be let down by such a physical blow? The immediate reaction to the news was one of disbelief. Billy was just two days short of his fifty-fifth birthday and, by today's standards, he was still a middle-aged man with plenty of life left.

It was a great cause for regret to Craig Brown that he was unable to attend the funeral, held on Thursday 11 December. He tried in vain to rearrange his busy schedule but found it totally impossible. It was also difficult for Manchester United boss Alex Ferguson to attend – but he managed to get there despite the fact that his side had been playing in Italy only the night before in an important European Champions' League match against Juventus. Ferguson had had little sleep but insisted on attending the funeral to pay his own respects to a man he had long admired.

There were many others who really would have liked to attend but were unable. Unfortunately, that is one of the problems of football – it is all-consuming. Commitments to see players and to play matches are plentiful and take priority, even over life and death. The game will not wait.

There was a touching floral tribute from fellow Scots and former Leeds players Gordon Strachan and Gary McAllister. Their message was simply, 'To Leeds United's greatest captain. It was an honour to follow in your footsteps.'

Fans turned up at Elland Road to tie their scarves and lay their flowers at the stadium, their own traditional way of showing how they felt about the loss of someone who had meant so much to them and their club. Suggestions were instantly mooted about a lasting tribute to Billy; Leeds United agreed that something should be done and a committee was set up to make the necessary arrangements.

It was hard to believe that Billy Bremner – *the* Billy Bremner – was no longer with us. For many that fact has still not really registered.

Billy Bremner was never truly lost to the game. At any given moment he would have answered the right call and gone off to manage a club somewhere. Just a few months before he died he told me that he was keeping his eye on the management vacancies. Hull City had interested him before Mark Hateley was appointed. A few months earlier, Grimsby Town's vacancy had also aroused his interest. He was not the sort of man to approach those clubs, though. It was not that he was proud or that he was playing hard to get either.

'I would not like to appear to be interfering,' he told me. 'It sounds a bit presumptuous to pick up the phone and say, "Hello, Billy Bremner here, I'm the answer to all your problems." It would put them in an embarrassing position and I would not want to do that.'

He was quite genuine. Off the pitch, Bremner was always a humble man. He seemed surprised if people even recognized him. He also had feelings for others. He was once at a dinner in Leeds where there was a former Manchester United player as guest speaker. The Manchester man was starting to get some stick from a handful of Leeds people who had, perhaps, had a few more drinks than they were capable of handling. Billy got to his feet and interrupted them.

'How would you like it if I was giving a talk in Manchester and got the sort of treatment you're giving this guy? I'll tell you something – I wouldn't like it! Now show a bit of respect to a man who was a bloody good footballer. If he walks out, I'm walking out alongside him.'

There was a deathly hush followed by applause. The Manchester man rose to his feet again and the applause continued. That incident showed that Billy Bremner had lost none of his bite – and none of his sense of justice.

For years after his retirement Billy continued to travel the length and breadth of Britain as a top after-dinner speaker; many of his engagements were no-fee charity appearances. He might travel from his home near Rotherham to Swansea, to Scotland, and back home again, all on consecutive days. His trusty Jaguar was his only companion for hours on end but he never felt like stopping.

'I'm flattered that people still want to meet me and to listen to what I have to say. I am also amazed because, when we were the Leeds United of Don Revie's day, we were not the most popular of teams by any means, and it surprises me that people are still talking to me after all these years.'

Yet talk to him they did. And they queued for autographs and stopped him in the street just to shake his hand. Billy Bremner remained a phenomenon right up to the day he died. Even afterwards, his image lived on. At his funeral the streets were lined with football supporters, many of them proudly holding up scarves they had worn years before when Billy was running the game at Elland Road. Driving through those streets to the St Mary's Roman Catholic Church in the little village of Edlington, you felt that it would take just one voice to motivate the entire mass of people to start shouting his name. They were there to pay homage, to make their own personal tribute, to rejoice in the memory of one of the greatest footballers who had ever lived.

Alex Smith and Allan Clarke both took part in the service, and even the officiating priest recalled seeing Billy score from forty yards in the 1970 European Cup semi-final between Leeds and Celtic. After the service the funeral cortège moved to Rose Hill Crematorium at Cantley – but there was a telling moment outside the church before the cars left as some of the biggest names in football mingled freely with the fans. There was no segregation, no fuss, just a common bond of being together to say farewell to Billy Bremner.

I once selected a brief verse of Rabbie Burns which I thought suited Billy's immense pride in being a Scot. Billy loved it:

My heart's in the Highlands, my heart is not here;
My heart's in the Highlands, a-chasing the deer.
Chasing the wild deer and following the roe,
My heart's in the Highlands, wherever I go.

That expressed how he felt about his homeland and his roots, but there have been other tributes to Billy. These are just a selected few.

JIMMY JOHNSTONE
'I was devastated when I heard that he was gone. He was a brilliant footballer and a great character. I laugh just thinking about some of his patter. His mind was always ticking over for something to have a laugh about.'

STUART McCALL
'I was a Leeds fan when I was a kid and Billy Bremner was always my inspiration. He tried to buy me twice when he was manager of Leeds and I was at Bradford City, but the club wouldn't let me go. To be considered by him to be good enough to want to sign me was a tremendous compliment.'

GARY McALLISTER
'I got to know him fairly well during my time at Elland Road. He was a real supporter, a genuine guy. I remember seeing him play in 1974 and I've watched footage of his career. He really was one helluva player.'

DAVE MACKAY
'When Billy went we lost one of the greatest Scottish players ever. He was a legend. You cannot manufacture the skill and toughness he had. His memory will live for ever.'

EDDIE GRAY

'It was absolutely tragic that he should go. Billy was a smashing fellow who I had known for a long, long time. He was a genuine friend.'

TERRY YORATH

To me he will always be a football legend. When Billy Bremner died we all lost someone very, very special.'

ALLAN CLARKE

'He was not just a team-mate and friend. He was like a brother to me, and even now there is not a day that goes by without me thinking about him.'

ALEX FERGUSON

'I always think of him as a man with great enthusiasm and a great player for Leeds and for Scotland. You can't put into words how much he meant to football.'

DAVID BATTY

'He was always great to me. He gave me my start in football. He was like a father to me and we used to speak to each other quite often – even years after we had parted company. I think he saw something of himself in me and I just hope that he knew how much I thought of him.'

BOBBY COLLINS

'Billy Bremner was nothing less than a truly great player. I remember him as a young boy and I remember him later in life. He had not changed a bit. He still loved life and he still loved football.'

ALEX SMITH

'He was what every young player wants to be – a successful master of his trade, honoured by his country, rewarded by the game and revered by his fellow players. Billy earned all that by sheer skill and determination. It made him a legend.'

JIMMY ARMFIELD

'I really thought of him as an inspirational footballer. No one doubted his talent or what a great skipper he was. He was always perky. What I loved about him was that he was the kind of player who could give a knock and take one, no matter what it was like, despite his small stature.

'We were not alike as people but I got on famously with him at Leeds. He would always give your side a lift. I think he was great at geeing people up. He was a great leader of the pack.'

NORMAN HUNTER

'I had been involved with the little fella for almost forty years. He had been a part of my life since I was fifteen. We were in digs together, played together, and were in management together. I just cannot believe that he is no longer with us.

'His great quality was that he loved the game, and that came over all the time. He just loved to play football and had this great desire. You don't get to be captain of Leeds United and Scotland without that.'

ELSIE REVIE

'Don and Billy were a pair – a footballing father and son in many ways. Everybody knew that. It doesn't seem right that both of them are gone at such comparatively young ages.'

PETER LORIMER

'We were a very close group of people at Leeds and we played together for a very long time. We came through as kids together and had great years at Leeds. We also roomed together when we were involved with Scotland.

'Billy enjoyed life but took his job very seriously. He was captain of Leeds and captain of Scotland and did both jobs magnificently.'

JACK CHARLTON

'He was a bundle of energy. Wherever the ball was you would find Billy there. He had a tremendous will to win and would always keep going right to the final whistle – and beyond it sometimes. He was the spirit of Leeds United.'

JIM BAXTER
'Billy was magnificent. Whether he was wearing a Leeds shirt, a Scotland shirt, or just joining in a practice game, he always played his heart out for his team. He was a one-off really. You just don't meet players like Billy Bremner more than once.'

CRAIG BROWN
'Billy Bremner was one of my personal heroes. He was a manager's dream, a great player and a tremendous influence on those around him. It was a great loss when he retired, and an even greater one when he passed away.'

DENIS LAW
'Bremner was a spectacular player. As an individual he was superb, as a team-mate he could inspire you to run through a brick wall. As an opponent he was best avoided. As a man he was a lovely guy. I'll always remember him in the Scotland dressing room winding everyone up. He's probably still doing it somewhere.'

TOMMY DOCHERTY
'I'll always remember asking him to be captain of Scotland. It was as if I were giving him the greatest Christmas present that he had ever had. But he had earned it. He was a great player and a marvellous captain.'

JOHNNY GILES
'He was a very energetic man. In a group of people he was the one cracking the jokes and getting everyone going. On the pitch he could do the unexpected and win games for you. He was very skilful and had great talent as well as the aggression which is needed in every player.'

KENNY DALGLISH
'Billy Bremner was a tremendous captain, a natural leader. He was tough and uncompromising, but he was also a terrific player with great skill to match his determination.'

ALAN HANSEN
'Players like Billy Bremner are very rare indeed. If you are lucky, they come along once in a lifetime. To me, though, he was unique – I can't even think of anyone else like him.'

NOBBY STILES
'We had some great tussles and you can't help respecting and admiring him. He was a tough customer but he could take it as well as dish it out. He was totally committed in every game he played, and you always knew you were in for a difficult match when he was in the opposition side. He was a tremendous asset to the game.'

MICK JONES
'Billy was a wonderful player and a fantastic captain. He never, ever threw the towel in. It didn't matter how important or unimportant the game was, he always gave it his best shot – and he made sure that the rest of us did too.'

CHARLIE NICHOLAS
'It must have been marvellous for Gordon McQueen and Joe Jordan when they were breaking into the Scotland team to have someone like Billy in the side. He was some player and will live on for ever as one of the greats of the game.'

BILLY McNEILL
'Towards the end of his life I did a few radio pieces with Billy and he was his usual effervescent self. He was in terrific form, enthusiastic about everything. Billy epitomized everything that we Scots are about. He had that fire and great enthusiasm. He put everything, his very soul, into all that he did. I loved the wee man.'

DAVID HAY

'I played with him in the 1974 World Cup and he was a great player and a great person. My strongest memories of Billy are from the game against Brazil in 1974, even though that match is recalled by many because Billy missed a chance to score. I was close to him when the ball came to him and it really wasn't much of a chance at all. The ball hit him and bounced off, rather than him playing it.'

As for me, he was everything that everyone else has said about him. I will always picture that shock of red hair darting about the pitch, and later the shorter silver hair atop a confident and warm smile, surrounded by his trophies and his most prized possession – his family.

... AND THE FINAL WORD

'Perhaps a lot of us will never go down in the memories of the fans as players who compare with the great individuals of the past. But I hope that I, at least, will be remembered as a member of a team which brought a long-awaited touch of glory to success-starved Leeds. I will be happy if that is the way it goes.'

Billy Bremner, 1974

INDEX